Contents

Introduction

What is a vegetarian?

Vegetarians never eat meat or fish or any products such as dripping, fish liver oils, gelatine, rennin or suet, which involve killing animals. But they do eat dairy foods because they are the natural produce of living creatures. Strict vegetarians, those belonging to the Vegan Society, refuse to eat any animal products at all. Instead of dairy foods, they use butter, cheese, cream and plant milks made from nuts and soya beans. Food reformers, although not vegetarians, also prefer the natural methods of food production, preparation and preservation. Their diet consists mainly of dairy products, fruit, nuts, vegetables, wholegrain cereals, yeasts and, occasionally, animal foods.

The vegetarian way of choosing food for health

Everyone needs food for four reasons: for *Vitality,* for *Building* a strong body and keeping it in good repair, *Muscular Energy* and for *Fun*.

Food for vitality

Vitality means being energetic and lively both in body and mind. It depends among other things on red blood, and to make red blood we need good supplies of iron and vitamin C in our food every day. Lack of iron and vitamin C causes anaemia which reduces the vitality of every living person, making them pale and possibly apathetic or slow-minded.

Good sources of iron are: almonds, black treacle, brazil and cashew nuts, cocoa, dried apricots, beans and figs, eggs, hazelnuts, lentils, peas, plain chocolate, sesame seeds, soya, sunflower seeds, walnuts, wheatgerm, yeast and yeast extracts, spices such as cumin and turmeric, and especially wholemeal cereals such as millet and oatmeal and enriched flour and bread.

The body loses a little iron each day which must be replaced. Anaemia builds up slowly when people live on diets just below requirements. Chemical laxatives can cause anaemia, even if you eat foods containing iron. Spinach and rhubarb reduce the amount of iron absorbed from food and therefore should be eaten sparingly. To prevent constipation drink plenty of liquids, especially vegetable and fruit juices, and eat about 25 g/1 oz bran per day.

Foods for building and keeping a strong body

The skeleton is the framework of the body. To make strong bones and teeth plenty of calcium is needed. Growing young people have a big need of calcium, and adults, too, need regular, though smaller supplies. This is because adults need calcium to renew and maintain strong bones. The original source is lime and chalk in the soil which is picked up by plants and animals. Calcium salts are added directly to food as in enriched flour and bread and also used in manufacturing processes.

The richest source of calcium is dried, skimmed milk. If adults took 40 g/1½ oz and teenagers 75 g/3 oz each day, their entire daily needs for calcium would be met. Besides milk, the following are rich in calcium: almond cream, almonds, beans, brazil nuts, broccoli, cheese (except cream cheese which is largely fat), coriander seeds, cumin seeds, dried figs, plant milks, also molasses, sesame seeds and paste (tahini), locust beans and wholegrain millet. Ensure enough calcium by taking daily 300 ml/½ pint of milk, 25 g/1 oz cheese and 40 g/1½ oz almonds or 40 g/1½ oz soya flour. Children and pregnant women need twice these amounts.

As well as needing enough calcium, we need sunshine or vitamin D in foods, to make strong bones and teeth. Vegetarians can get good supplies of natural vitamin D from eggs and some from butter, and synthetic vitamin D in enriched baby foods, evaporated milk, margarine and vegetarian milks. Spinach is very rich in calcium but strangely enough, less calcium and iron is absorbed from foods if spinach and rhubarb are eaten. Wholegrain products and pulses also contain a substance which spoils calcium absorption, but vegetarians who eat soaked pulses and cereals, use yeast and malt in cooking, get plenty of sunshine and enough vitamin D, are well protected against its effects.

To build muscles, flesh and body tissues, protein is needed. The best building foods are cheese, eggs and milk because they contain plenty of protein of the right quality. These foods may seem expensive, but are good value because they have such concentrated food value that they can be used in small quantities, combined with cereals, pulses and nuts, to produce mixtures of high growth value, for example pizzas and risottos and nutmeals.

Lacto-vegetarians have no problems with protein, but strict vegetarians and some people in under-developed countries have to rely on vegetable foods and carefully chosen mixtures of cereals, green leaves, nuts, pulses, seeds and yeast to supply enough. Soya flour and almonds have almost equal protein value to dried milk and cheese: the Chinese have relied on soya beans instead of dairy produce for centuries. Modern food technology is helping all vegetarians by producing new 'building mixtures' especially for infants. Some of these are used by Oxfam and UNICEF and some are sold in health food shops.

Vitamin C is required for building too. It is essential for making the cement or connective tissue that binds skin, flesh, muscles and bones firmly together, making the body tissues firm and well-knit. Foods rich in vitamin C include blackcurrant syrup, Brussels sprouts, cabbage, cauliflower, citrus fruits, cress, peppers, rosehip syrup, swedes, tomatoes and watercress. Ensure enough vitamin C with a daily intake of 1 orange or 150 ml/¼ pint of citrus fruit juice.

Foods for muscular energy

Working muscles need fuel foods and especially thiamine (vitamin B_1) to produce muscular energy and warmth from the fuel foods. Fuel foods include flour, potatoes, rice, sugar and tapioca. Thiamine acts like the match that lights a fire. If lacking in thiamine, fuel foods are as useless as an unlit fire for energy and warmth.

Rich sources of thiamine include yeast, fresh peanuts, hazelnuts, sesame seeds, sesame paste (tahini), soya beans, soya flour, sunflower seeds, wheatgerm and yeast extracts. Good sources are: almonds, bread, buckwheat, cashew nuts, cheese, eggs, millet, milk, oatmeal, wheat, whole barley and all kinds of flour except rice flour. Fresh and frozen peas, broccoli and most green and root vegetables also supply small but useful amounts of thiamine to the diet.

Niacin or nicotinic acid is another B vitamin. It is essential for muscular activity and stamina, and the proper functioning of the digestive tract and the skin. Many of the foods listed as good sources of thiamine are also good sources of niacin: coffee, mushrooms, peanuts, peanut butter and tea are especially good sources. Thiamine in foods is lost or reduced by heat, by solubility in water, long, slow cooking, keeping hot or reheating and by the effects of baking soda and baking powder. To retain thiamine, choose quick preparation methods, use little water and as little cooking as possible. Pulses should be soaked and then pressure-cooked or steamed, cereals cooked so that water is absorbed and not thrown away, nuts pounded, doughs and pancakes raised with yeast and vegetables cut small and cooked quickly.

Ensure enough thiamine by eating daily, 175 g/6 oz bread, and 50 g/2 oz oatmeal (weighed dry) or 25 g/1 oz wheatgerm, as well as greens and yeast extract.

Fun foods

These include arrowroot, cornflour, gherkins, jams, most sweets and syrup. They have little or no food value as sources of material for muscular energy, growth or vitality, but are useful to stimulate the appetite and make nourishing foods attractive and fun to eat.

Daily food needs for lacto-vegetarians

Adults need:

175 g/6 oz bread
25 g /1 oz cheese
5 g/¼ oz cocoa or
    25 g/1 oz plain chocolate
1 egg
300 ml/½ pint milk
125 ml/4 fl oz orange juice
    or 1 fresh orange
25 g/1 oz bran or
    50 g/2 oz oatmeal
1 serving fresh vegetables,
    raw or cooked

Children and teenagers need:

300 g/10 oz bread
50 g/2 oz cheese
5 g/¼ oz cocoa or
    25 g/1 oz plain chocolate
1 egg
600 ml/1 pint milk
125 ml/4 fl oz orange juice
    or 1 fresh orange
25 g/1 oz bran or
    50 g/2 oz oatmeal
1 serving fresh vegetables,
    raw or cooked

In addition adults need about 250 g/8 oz enriched margarine a week, children about 500 g/1 lb. Nuts, soya flour, yeast and yeast extract should be eaten frequently.

Daily food needs for vegans

Adults need:

75 g/3 oz almonds or brazil nuts
  or 15 g/½ oz sesame seeds
175 g/6 oz bread

5 g/¼ oz cocoa or
  25 g/1 oz plain chocolate
300 ml/½ pint enriched
  vegetarian milk
125 ml/4 fl oz orange juice or
  1 fresh orange
50 g/2 oz soya flour
25 g/1 oz bran or
  50 g/2 oz oatmeal
1 serving fresh vegetables,
  raw or cooked

Children and teenagers need:

75 g/3 oz almonds or brazil nuts
  or 15 g/½ oz sesame seeds
300 g/10 oz mixed bread or
  250 g/8 oz brown bread
5 g/¼ oz cocoa or
  25 g/1 oz plain chocolate
600 ml/1 pint enriched
  vegetarian milk
125 ml/4 fl oz orange juice or
  1 fresh orange
50 g/2 oz soya flour
25 g/1 oz bran or
  50 g/2 oz oatmeal
1 serving fresh vegetables,
  raw or cooked

Plus, weekly, enriched margarine, green vegetables, pulses and yeast.

These amounts of vital foods cover basic bodily needs for growth, repair, energy and vitality. Most people will add on fuel foods such as biscuits, cakes, chips, pastry and sugar, to keep their weight steady.

How to use the list of daily food needs

Use it to plan the food budget. Calculate total weekly amounts and then the cost. For example, a family of four (two adults and two children) will need 1.25 kg/2½ lb cheese and five 625 g/20 oz cans orange juice a week.

Use it to plan meals, checking that the foods listed above are included.

Use it to check your diet. Have you eaten the vital foods?

Food storage equipment

This is important for fresh food and economy. Cold storage equipment makes shopping easier and keeps food fresh. To take advantage of bargains in supermarkets, cold storage conditions are essential.

A cool, dry store cupboard with narrow 12-cm/5-inch shelves taking single rows of cans, jars or packets. All groceries, even canned and processed foods, keep best in a cool store, rather than a warm kitchen cupboard where they may lose their vitamin value.
A refrigerator as large as possible and with plenty of large containers with tight lids to keep fruit and vegetables fresh.
A deep freezer, preferably a cupboard model or chest with a top opening and use a thermometer to check the temperature, which must be at −18°C/0°F. Store freshly baked bread, doughs, prepared fruit and vegetables, ready cooked dishes, pastry and soups, all tightly wrapped in special, heavy gauge polythene and closed to keep air-tight.

Some special problems in the preparation of vegetarian foods

Vegetarian foods are apt to be bulky and too satisfying and give a full feeling after meals. This is because they contain fibre (cellulose), especially in wholegrain cereals, pulses, nuts and also more water, especially in vegetables and fruits, than in other foods. Nuts and pulses have a close texture which makes them slow to digest.

Some vegetarian foods are more digestible and less bulky if they are puréed, mashed, chopped or shredded. Nuts should be milled, crushed or ground to a cream. Pulses need soaking and cooking until soft and tender. The texture of wholegrain doughs can be made lighter and more digestible by using yeast and eggs.

Store soaked, raw pulses in the freezer. Cook as for frozen peas and beans.

Giving a good flavour to vegetarian foods

The flavour of meat is proverbial and stimulates the appetite and flow of digestive juices. The savour arises from natural components present in meat. One of these is glutamic acid which also occurs in wheat, soya and many other plant proteins. Proteins can be hydrolyzed to give monosodium glutamate which is used to intensify meat and vegetable flavours. The Chinese have been doing this for centuries as soy sauce, which is on every table in Chinese restaurants to add a savoury taste to foods.

Modern food technology is producing a wide variety of savoury tastes from hydrolyzed proteins of yeast. In addition to the yeast extracts, which are valuable for B vitamins as well as for flavour, there are the specific savoury flavours such as bacon and chicken which are wholly vegetarian in origin. Seasoned salt, seasoned pepper and garlic salt are useful seasonings to buy.

Good savoury flavours can also be produced in food by careful cooking and seasoning. Celery, mushrooms and onions, cooked gently with fat and seasoned with salt, produce an especially savoury taste which contains glutamate from the vegetables and seasoning. The following list of herbs, spices and flavourings used in the recipes gives an idea of the most suitable ones to have in stock in your kitchen.

Dried vegetables: celery flakes, dried onion and mushrooms.

Dried herbs: in addition to mixed herbs, keep basil, marjoram, sage and thyme.

Fresh herbs: these are worth growing in pots or window boxes – chives, dill, fennel, marjoram, mint, parsley, sage and thyme.

Dried spices: cloves, cinnamon, coriander, cumin seeds, ginger, ground mace, peppercorns and whole nutmeg.

Fresh spices: coriander and curry leaves.

Green ginger: this gives a particularly fresh taste to vegetables, savoury and sweet dishes. To keep it fresh, store in a screw-top jar in the refrigerator.

Garlic bulbs: these should be stored in an airy, dry place, not in a closed container or they will go mouldy. Cut garlic will keep in a mixture of oil and salt in an open jar in the kitchen or in a tightly covered jar in the refrigerator.

Sea salt: comes in coarse crystals and has a stronger flavour than ordinary table salt. It is especially nice with buttered jacket potatoes.

Sauces: soy, tomato and Worcestershire.

Making foods appetizing

Good food should be made to look and taste appetizing so that it is enjoyable as well as nutritive. Garnishes and flavourings stimulate the appetite and flow of digestive juices, resulting in better digestion and nutrition.

Garnishes:

Yellow garnishes: bananas, hard-boiled eggs, lemons, orange slices and twists, pineapple rings or cubes and raw or cooked carrot.

Green garnishes: cooked peas, cucumber slices or twists, green peppers, small bunches of mustard and cress, olives and sprigs of watercress or parsley.

Red garnishes: cherries, corralline pepper, paprika, red cabbage, canned or fresh red peppers and tomatoes.

Black garnishes: fried and pickled mushrooms, black olives, pickled prunes, truffles, pickled walnuts.

Why be a vegetarian?

A lacto-vegetarian diet is considered by many nutritionists to be the best diet for health. Animal foods such as meat and fish add variety, but not always better food value, to the diet.

Because the processes of rearing and slaughtering animals are repugnant to many people, they prefer a vegetarian diet. Some people believe that flesh eating has spiritual effects and like some Hindus and Buddhists, have religious reasons for being vegetarian.

The Vegetarian Society was founded in Manchester in 1847. Its aims were to 'promote the use of cereals, pulses, vegetables and fruit as articles of diet, and induce habits of abstinence from fish, flesh and fowl'. The Society urged that a vegetarian diet would support a larger population and thus render Britain independent of foreign food supplies.

'That it is favourable to temperance and a peaceful disposition, that its adoption is economical and enables people to live better, that it stops the horrors of the slaughter house and that man originally lived on a vegetable diet.' Some of these arguments have been disproved, others have an old-fashioned ring, although it is still true that a piece of land produces more food if used to grow plants than it does if rearing animals for food.

Animals supply only 10% (as meat), 15% (as eggs) and 30% (as milk) of the food value of the plants and vegetables they eat. So a vegetarian diet is the quickest and best answer to the present world food shortage, especially if cooks and technologists can make it tasty and attractive as well as yielding good food value. Vegetarian dishes can be nutritious, and appetizing and fun to eat, and that is the reason for this book.

Notes on ingredients for vegetarian cooking

Since many cheeses contain animal rennet, strict vegetarians may wish to use vegetarian cheeses in recipes using cheese. Ask at your local supermarket or health food shop for cheeses containing a vegetarian rennet. Vegetarian Cheddar is widely available.

Parmesan is not vegetarian, but Pecorino is a suitable substitute. Danish Blue has a vegetarian alternative. Among English cheeses, there are no vegetarian alternatives for Derby or sage Derby. Strict vegetarians may wish to avoid recipes containing these cheeses or to experiment with their own alternatives.

Vegetarians will generally use only free-range eggs in dishes, avoiding battery or barn varieties. The seaweed product agar agar can be used in place of gelatine and a vegetarian version of Worcestershire sauce is available. Butter is suitable for vegetarians, but because of its high saturated fat content, a healthier vegetable variety, such as sunflower margarine, may be used.

Health foods and vegetarian foods

The following is a small selection of the wide range of products available at any health food store.

Breakfast cereals
barley; biscuit cereals; bran; maize; millet; muesli; oats and oatflakes – various brands

Wholemeal flours, meals and grains
flours: Allinson wholemeal
meal: millet; oatmeal; rye meal – various brands, some health food shops provide their own
grains: barley; buckwheat; millet; rye; whole unground wheat – various brands, some health food shops provide their own.

Wheatgerm
Bemax; Froment

Oils, fats and creams
oils: corn oil; groundnut oil; safflower seed oil; sesame seed oil; soya oil
fats: Granose

creams: creamed coconut, Granose soya cream
nut butters: almond; cashew nut; hazelnut; peanut; tahini

Yeasts and yeast extracts
yeast: Allinson active baking yeast/easy bake yeast
extracts: Barmene; Marmite; Natex; Vecon

Savoury extracts
soy sauce; tamari

Savoury spreads and pâtés
Tartex

Salad dressings
cider vinegar; Honegar

Glutamate powders
Marigold

Savoury nut mixes
Sasmix; Realeat

Tinned nut meats
Nuttolene; Sausalatas

Milk products
Granose; Plamil soya milk

Salts
Herbamare; sea salt

Soya beans and products:
soya beans; soya flour – various brands, many health food shops
provide their own

Gelatine substitute
Gelozone; agar agar

Appetizers, Spreads and Dips

Norwegian Appetizer

METRIC/IMPERIAL

2 tablespoons double cream
1 tablespoon lemon juice
a little grated lemon rind
salt and sugar to taste
1 x 5-cm/2-inch piece
  cucumber, peeled and diced
1 medium-sized cooking
  apple, peeled and diced

3 whole spring onions, or
  1 small onion and some
  chives, finely chopped
few sprigs raw cauliflower
lemon twist
little cress

Mix together cream, lemon juice and rind, salt and sugar. Stir in vegetables. Serve piled in a dish, or in individual dishes, garnished with lemon twist and cress.

Serves 6

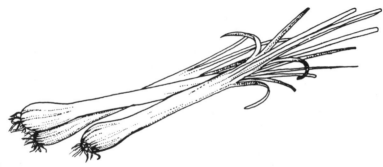

Cauliflower à la Grecque

METRIC/IMPERIAL

2 large sprigs thyme or 2 level
   teaspoons dried thyme
150 ml/¼ pint dry white wine
150 ml/¼ pint fruity olive oil
75 ml/⅛ pint lemon juice
1 bay leaf
1 level teaspoon salt

2 level teaspoons white
   peppercorns, lightly crushed
1 level teaspoon coriander
   seeds, lightly crushed
500 g/1 lb cauliflower, broken
   into small sprigs
little chopped parsley

If using dried thyme, tie in a little piece of muslin.

Collect wine, oil, lemon, herbs and spices in a saucepan. Bring to the boil. Drop in cauliflower sprigs. Cover and simmer for about 25 minutes. Add a little more wine if liquid is too much reduced.

Cool the pickle in the pan and keep in covered dish in refrigerator.

Serve cold, sprinkled with parsley.

Serves 8

NOTE: Other suitable vegetables for serving à la Grecque are: sliced or diced aubergines, fresh or canned artichoke hearts, strips of white fennel root, celeriac, celery sticks, cucumber and mushrooms.

Iced Tomato Starter

METRIC/IMPERIAL

300 ml/½ pint milk
1 x 300 g/10 oz can tomato
   soup
1 x 300 g/10 oz can tomato
   juice

2 teaspoons tomato purée
dash Worcestershire sauce
salt and pepper to taste
pinch chopped parsley or
   chives

Blend together first six ingredients. Chill. Before serving, add parsley or chives.

Serves 6

Mushrooms with Sour Cream

METRIC/IMPERIAL

1 small onion, finely chopped
25 g/1 oz butter
2 tablespoons milk
1 teaspoon flour
250 g/8 oz mushrooms,
    washed and sliced

150 ml/¼ pint sour cream
salt, pepper and paprika to
    taste

Fry onion in butter over low heat until golden. Stir in the milk, blended with flour. Boil. Add the mushrooms and half the sour cream.

Simmer until mushrooms are tender. Season with salt, pepper and paprika.

Stir in the rest of the sour cream. Serve hot or cold.

Serves 4

Hungarian Salata

METRIC/IMPERIAL

1 onion, chopped
1 carrot, thinly sliced
2 tablespoons olive oil
2 red or green peppers, seeded
250 g/8 oz red or green
    tomatoes, skinned and cut
    into quarters

1 clove garlic, finely chopped
pinch salt and black pepper
2 teaspoons lemon juice or
    vinegar
little chopped parsley

Lightly fry onion and carrot in oil for 5 minutes in a covered, thick pan. Add peppers. Cook 5 minutes longer. Add tomatoes and garlic. Cook covered over moderate heat, shaking frequently, until carrot is just tender. Season with salt and pepper. Add lemon juice or vinegar.

Chill. Sprinkle with parsley and serve with toast.

Serves 4

Vinaigrette Dressings for Mixed Vegetable Hors d'Oeuvre

Garlic
1 large clove garlic
½ level teaspoon salt
1 level teaspoon sugar
1 level teaspoon French
    mustard
150 ml/¼ pint olive oil
2 tablespoons vinegar
pinch freshly ground black
    pepper

Plain
½ level teaspoon salt
1 level teaspoon sugar

1 level teaspoon dry mustard
150 ml/¼ pint olive oil
2 tablespoons vinegar or
    lemon juice
black pepper to taste

Curry
½ level teaspoon salt
1 level teaspoon sugar
1–2 level teaspoons curry
    powder
150 ml/¼ pint vegetable oil
juice and grated rind of ½ small
    lemon

Crush seasonings with a wooden spoon in a bowl or in a pestle and mortar. Mix in the oil and then vinegar or lemon juice to taste. Transfer to small screw-topped glass jars and store in refrigerator.

Serves 6

Vegetables

4–6 thinly sliced young mushrooms without stalks. Mix with garlic vinaigrette and chopped chives or plain vinaigrette, using lemon juice and adding chopped parsley.

125 g/4 oz seeded, thinly sliced red or green peppers, mixed with garlic or plain dressing and chopped chives or onion garnish.

125 g/4 oz cooked or canned small broad beans (drained) mixed with garlic or plain vinaigrette and plenty of chopped parsley.

125 g/4 oz sliced raw young broad beans mixed with vinaigrette and parsley.

50 g/2 oz raw, very thinly sliced white fennel root. Mixed with plain dressing – use parsley for garnish.

125 g/4 oz skinned, sliced, firm, small tomatoes. Mixed with plain dressing and sprinkled with chopped fresh tarragon or thyme or thinly sliced onion rings.

125 g/4 oz cooked or canned asparagus (drained). Mixed with plain vinaigrette.

125 g/4 oz cauliflower sprigs, boiled one minute, drained and cooled. Mixed with curry dressing and garnished with chives.

125 g/4 oz raw, thinly sliced young carrots, cut into matchsticks, and thinly sliced celery sticks. Mix with curry dressing and chopped chives.

125 g/4 oz thinly sliced young French beans, boiled 5 minutes, drained and cooled. Mix with plain vinaigrette.

125 g/4 oz small new potatoes, boiled unpeeled, skinned, cooled and mixed with curry dressing and chopped chives or spring onion tops.

Raw sweetcorn, off the cob, and spring onion. Mix with chopped spring onions and plain dressing made with lemon juice and 1 tablespoon of thin cream added.

125 g/4 oz sliced celeriac or a thick celery root, boiled 5 minutes, cooled and cut in thin strips. Mix with plain dressing and garnish with chopped chives or pinch paprika.

125 g/4 oz red cabbage, sliced very finely off the top of a small red cabbage, thus avoiding the stalks. Mix with plain dressing and garnish with radishes. The rest of the cabbage can be cooked or pickled.

Mock Caviar

METRIC/IMPERIAL

500 g/1 lb aubergines (about 2 large ones)
1 large clove garlic, crushed with 1 level teaspoon salt
2 shallots, finely chopped
2 tablespoons finely chopped green pepper

pepper and paprika to taste
little lemon juice
2–3 tablespoons fruity olive oil
few black olives
few lemon slices
2 tomatoes, chopped

Bake aubergines, whole, at 180°C/350°F, Gas Mark 4, for 40 minutes.

Cool. Split and scrape out pulp with wooden spoon into bowl. Rub the black skin through a coarse wire sieve or chop very finely. Mix in the next eight ingredients. Chill thoroughly.

Put in a pottery bowl and garnish with black olives, lemon slices and tomatoes. Serve with black rye or brown bread and butter or with crispbread.

Serves 4

Egg Pâté

METRIC/IMPERIAL

1 large tin Tartex (90 g/3½ oz)
75 g/3 oz unsalted butter
2 hard-boiled eggs, roughly chopped

cayenne pepper to taste
lemon juice to taste

Mix all ingredients together. Serve as for Almond Pâté (page 22).

Serves 4

Almond Pâté

METRIC/IMPERIAL

75 g/3 oz unsalted butter
1 large tin Tartex (90 g/3½ oz)
50 g/2 oz ground almonds
25 g/1 oz salted almonds,
   finely chopped

freshly ground black pepper to
   taste
4 stuffed olives, sliced
cucumber twist
4 lettuce leaves (optional)

Cream the butter and work in the Tartex and almonds to make a smooth paste. Add a little freshly ground black pepper.

Press into pâté jar or pottery dish. Smooth the top and mark with a fork. Garnish with olives and cucumber twist. Chill.

Serve from the jar or, in rounded spoonfuls on lettuce leaves on individual plates, topped with olives.

Serves 4

Pâté Fines Herbes

METRIC/IMPERIAL

1 large tin Tartex (90 g/3½ oz)
50–75 g/2–3 oz unsalted butter
2–3 tablespoons chives, finely
   chopped
1 tablespoon parsley, finely
   chopped

½ tablespoon thyme, finely
   chopped
few sprigs cress
lemon twist

Mix Tartex and butter together. Work in the herbs. Shape to a flat round. Coat sides with parsley or press into a pâté pot.

Serve, garnished with cress and lemon twist, with toast or crispbread.

Serves 4–5

NOTE: If using dried herbs, leave overnight for flavour to develop.

VARIATION: Add mildly flavoured grated cheese or cottage cheese and butter.

Yogurt

METRIC/IMPERIAL

*600 ml/1 pint milk, boiled,
cooled, or sterilized milk*
*2 heaped tablespoons milk
powder or 150 ml/¼ pint
evaporated milk*

*3 teaspoons fresh natural
yogurt (bought or home-
made)*

In a large bowl, whisk together milk, milk powder or
evaporated milk and yogurt. Pour into small pots or jars,
which have been well rinsed after washing in running hot
water. (Detergent traces will spoil yogurt.)

Place pots of milk, standing in hot water, in a large shallow
saucepan. Cover and leave overnight, preferably standing the
pot in a warm, but not hot place, such as over the pilot light
on your stove. Or place the yogurt jars in a large dry
saucepan, cover with lid and stand in the airing cupboard. If
not quite set in the morning, stand pots in fresh hot water and
leave another hour.

When set, store the yogurt in the refrigerator, covered. Use
this to make your next batch.

NOTE: Buy a fresh carton of natural yogurt every week as home-made yogurt
tends to become weaker and not taste so good. If the yogurt is rather sour,
use only 2 teaspoons to make the next batch.

Soured yogurts can be used for salad dressing, making scones (1 level
teaspoon bicarbonate of soda to 250 g/8 oz plain flour mixed with 4
tablespoons yogurt) or to make bread. Soured yogurt will make a creamy
cottage cheese with a specially smooth texture.

Salata Yogurt

METRIC/IMPERIAL
3 cartons natural yogurt
75–125 g/3–4 oz salata

squeeze lemon juice
few sprigs watercress

Mix drained salata with yogurt. Add lemon juice to taste. Chill and serve in hors d'œuvres dishes, garnished with watercress.

Serves 4

Tangy Yogurt

METRIC/IMPERIAL
150 ml/¼ pint (1 carton) natural
*   yogurt*
50 g/2 oz pickled cucumber or
*   gherkin, chopped*

8 capers, chopped
8 olives, stoned or stuffed,
*   chopped*
few drops green colouring

Mix all ingredients together. Colour lightly with a skewer dipped into green colouring.

Chill and serve in glasses on top of shredded lettuce, with toast or crispbread.

Serves 2

Yogurt Hors d'Oeuvre

METRIC/IMPERIAL
150 ml/¼ pint natural yogurt
1 shallot, finely chopped
25 g/1 oz red pepper, seeded
*   and finely chopped*

1 stick celery, finely chopped
50 g/2 oz tomatoes, skinned,
*   seeded and chopped*
garlic salt to taste

Combine all ingredients. Chill and serve.

Serves 2

Basic Spread Mix

METRIC/IMPERIAL

250 g/8 oz butter or margarine
50 g/2 oz soya flour or ground
    almonds

2 tablespoons boiling water

Cream the butter or margarine. Add soya flour or almonds and water. Beat until smooth and creamy, using a wooden spoon.

Serves 5

VARIATIONS:
Curry Spread: Add to 50 g/2 oz basic spread, 2–3 tablespoons curry powder or paste, 1 teaspoon yeast extract, juice and rind of ½ lemon and 15 g/½ oz grated coconut cream or peanut butter.
Nutty Spread: Add to 50–75 g/2–3 oz basic spread, 50 g/2 oz chopped or minced salted almonds, ¼ vegetable stock cube, pinch nutmeg and squeeze lemon juice.
Creamy Cheese Spread: Beat into 50–75 g/2–3 oz basic spread, 125 g/4 oz grated mild cheese, 2 teaspoons lemon juice or vinegar and pepper to taste.
Egg Spread: Combine 50–75 g/2–3 oz basic spread mix with 2 teaspoons yeast or savoury extract or ¼ vegetable stock cube. Mix in 2 chopped hard-boiled eggs.

Curried Beans Spread

METRIC/IMPERIAL

1 x 250 g/8 oz can curried
    beans
1 tablespoon milk powder or
    soya flour

125 g/4 oz dry cheese, grated
1 tablespoon sweet pickle

Mash beans in sauce and mix in dried milk or soya flour and enough cheese to make a smooth paste. Mix in sweet pickle to taste.

Serves 4

VARIATIONS: For a stronger flavour, add more curry paste; 2 teaspoons curry powder fried in 1 tablespoon oil with a little onion or 1 teaspoon fresh ginger, finely chopped.

For more food value, add 25 g/1 oz chopped hard-boiled egg and 1 teaspoon yeast extract.

Sherry Dip

METRIC/IMPERIAL

250 g/8 oz cream cheese
2 tablespoons sherry
1 tablespoon double cream
25 g/1 oz walnuts, finely
   chopped

pinch curry powder
8 olives, stoned and chopped

Blend all ingredients together to a smooth paste.

Serves 6–8

Paprika Dip

METRIC/IMPERIAL

50 g/2 oz unsalted butter,
   creamed
50 g/2 oz cottage cheese
125 g/4 oz Gorgonzola

2–3 teaspoons paprika
1 teaspoon Worcestershire
   sauce
2–3 tablespoons salad cream

Cream butter with wooden spoon. Beat in cottage cheese, then Gorgonzola and seasoning. Whisk in salad cream until light and fluffy.

Serve with potato crisps for dipping.

Serves 8

Savoury Cheese Spread

METRIC/IMPERIAL

1 x 250 g/8 oz can baked
   beans in tomato sauce
125–175 g/4–6 oz dry cheese,
   grated
pepper to taste

Mash beans in sauce with a fork in a bowl. Work in enough cheese to make a smooth, thick paste. Season with pepper. Spread thickly on hot buttered toast.

Serves 4–6

NOTE: For a stronger flavour mix in a little yeast extract.

Cucumber Dip

METRIC/IMPERIAL

1 x 2.5-cm/1-inch piece
  unpeeled cucumber, finely
  chopped
½ level teaspoon salt
175–250 g/6–8 oz cream
  cheese
1 teaspoon onion, finely
  chopped

½ teaspoon Worcestershire
  sauce
1 teaspoon lemon juice
garlic salt to taste
few drops green colouring
little cress

Sprinkle cucumber with salt. Let stand for 5 minutes.

Mash cheese with wooden spoon in bowl to a smooth paste. Work in cucumber, onion, Worcestershire sauce and lemon juice. Add garlic salt. Dip a skewer into green colouring and colour mixture pale green. Garnish with cress.

Serves 6

Welsh Dip

METRIC/IMPERIAL

1 packet leek soup
300 ml/½ pint sour cream
50 g/2 oz grated cheese

dash paprika or few chopped
  chives

Mix all ingredients together and beat well. Chill for at least 2–3 hours in covered dish. Sprinkle paprika or chives on top just before serving.

Serves 8

NOTE: Soured cream can be bought, or made at home by mixing one carton each of natural yogurt and double or canned cream.

VARIATION: Use 1 packet celery soup instead of leek soup and add 25 g/1 oz finely chopped walnuts.

Spicy Peanut Dip

METRIC/IMPERIAL
150 ml/¹/₄ pint natural yogurt
1 rounded tablespoon peanut
  butter
50 g/2 oz cheese, grated
1 level tablespoon green or red
  pepper, finely chopped

1 clove garlic, crushed with 1
  level teaspoon salt
pinch chilli powder
1–2 level teaspoons curry
  powder
little lemon juice

Combine all ingredients in a bowl and beat to a creamy consistency. Thin with a little water and lemon juice if needed. Serve with crisps, savoury biscuits and toast fingers.

Serves 6

African Dip

METRIC/IMPERIAL
25 g/1 oz coconut cream,
  coarsely grated
2 tablespoons boiling water
1 heaped tablespoon peanut
  butter, smooth or crunchy
1 tablespoon onion, finely
  chopped

grated rind and juice of
  ¹/₂ small lemon
1 heaped tablespoon dried
  milk or soya flour
1 x 5-mm/¹/₄-inch piece fresh
  chilli, finely chopped

Melt coconut cream in boiling water. Add peanut butter, onion, lemon juice and rind, and beat in enough dried milk or soya flour to make a thick cream. Beat well to make it light. Add chilli.

Serve in a bowl with potato and Coconut Crisps (see page 248).

Serves 6

Creamy Onion Dip

METRIC/IMPERIAL

300 ml/ ½ pint double cream
1–2 tablespoons onion soup mix

1–2 teaspoons lemon juice

Blend the cream with a tablespoon of onion soup mix and a teaspoon of lemon juice. Add more onion soup mix and lemon juice to taste.

Serves 8

Salsa Verde (Green Sauce)

METRIC/IMPERIAL

2 heaped tablespoons
  chopped parsley
1 tablespoon chopped mint
1 tablespoon grated
  horseradish

2 tablespoons white
  breadcrumbs
3 tablespoons olive oil
1 level teaspoon salt
little lemon juice

Pound all ingredients together in a pestle and mortar to make a thick green sauce.

Serves 6

Tahini Dip

METRIC/IMPERIAL

2 heaped tablespoons tahini
  (sesame paste)
1 clove garlic crushed with ½
  level teaspoon salt

1–2 tablespoons parsley, finely
  chopped
2–3 tablespoons lemon juice
little water if necessary

Mix all ingredients together, adding a little water if needed, to make a smooth cream. Serve with toast, crisps, celery or cucumber slices.

Serves 4

NOTE: Sesame seeds are extremely rich in thiamine, calcium and iron.

Guacamole

METRIC/IMPERIAL

2 avocados, peeled and
  mashed
1 level teaspoon fresh red
  chilli, finely chopped or ½
  level teaspoon chilli powder
2–3 tablespoons olive oil

little salt
1–2 tablespoons lemon juice
1 small onion, finely chopped
few strips red pepper, thinly
  sliced or few lemon twists
  and few tomato twists

Mash avocados with chilli, olive oil and lemon juice. Add as much oil as can be absorbed. Salt to taste. Fold in onion.

Serve, chilled, in a pottery or wooden bowl, garnished with lemon and tomato twists or red pepper strips.

Serves 4–5

Il Pesto

METRIC/IMPERIAL

25 g/1 oz nuts (pine kernels,
  cashew nuts or almonds)
50 g/2 oz fresh herbs (basil,
  marjoram, thyme or parsley)
25 g/1 oz cheese (Parmesan,
  Caerphilly or Cheddar with a
  touch of Danish Blue)

1–2 cloves garlic
4–5 tablespoons olive oil
salt to taste

Pound all ingredients together to a smooth paste in a pestle and mortar. Rub through a wire strainer or use a liquidizer to make a smoother paste.

Serve cold as a dip or hot as a sauce for pasta, an addition to soups, or a topping for jacket potatoes.

Serves 4

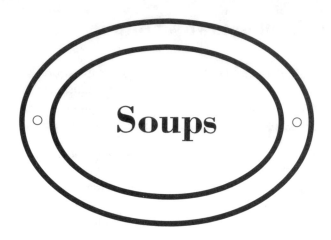

Country Soup from Provence

METRIC/IMPERIAL

500 g/1 lb potatoes, peeled and diced
500 g/1 lb onions, sliced
50 g/2 oz butter or 4 tablespoons oil
10 sage leaves, chopped or 2 level teaspoons dried sage
2 cloves of garlic, chopped
1.8 litres/3 pints water

1 level tablespoon salt
½ level tablespoon cornflour blended with 150 ml/¼ pint evaporated milk
1 level teaspoon pepper
pinch chopped chives or green leek leaves
Forcemeat Balls (see page 47).

Fry vegetables, sage and garlic in oil or butter, stirring frequently, for 5 minutes over low heat in a saucepan. Pour in water and salt. Simmer until tender. This will take 30 minutes in a saucepan, or 5 minutes in a pressure cooker.

Stir in cornflour and milk and boil to thicken. Correct the seasoning. Serve in a tureen, garnished with chopped chives or green leek leaves and fried sage and onion Forcemeat Balls (see page 47).

Serves 6

White Mulligatawny Soup

METRIC/IMPERIAL

1 medium-sized onion, finely
  chopped
25 g/1 oz margarine or nut fat
2 tablespoons vegetable oil
1–2 level tablespoons curry
  powder
1 level tablespoon cornflour
900 ml/1 ½ pints vegetable
  stock or water and yeast
  extract
2 level tablespoons ground
  almonds

1 level tablespoon soya flour
1 level tablespoon jelly
  marmalade or sugar
1 tablespoon lemon juice
1 egg
2 tablespoons evaporated milk
  (optional)
salt to taste
few chopped chives or
  chopped spring onion

Fry onion in fat and oil until pale yellow. Add curry powder and cornflour. Then stir in water and yeast extract or stock and boil to thicken.

Add almonds and soya flour, blended with a little water. Stir in jelly marmalade or sugar and lemon juice and simmer for 45 minutes. Rub through a strainer. Reheat.

Beat egg and mix with milk in a large casserole or tureen. Pour in hot soup and add salt. Garnish with chives or spring onion.

Serves 4

Gazpacho

METRIC/IMPERIAL

2 large slices bread, trimmed
2 cloves garlic, crushed
1 teaspoon salt
2 tablespoons lemon juice
150 ml/¹/₄ pint water
150 ml/¹/₄ pint olive oil
1 x 15-cm/6-inch piece
  cucumber, peeled and
  coarsely grated

1 green pepper, seeded and
  finely chopped
1 medium-sized onion, finely
  chopped
1 x 625 g/20 oz can tomatoes

Pound bread, garlic, salt, lemon juice, water and oil to a paste in a pestle and mortar.

Put the bread mix, 150 g/5 oz cucumber, green pepper, onion, and 575 g/19 oz tomatoes (rubbed through a nylon strainer to remove pips) in a large basin.

If possible pass through a vegetable grater to make a purée. Season. Add more cold water if too thick. Chill. Serve garnished with remaining cucumber and tomato.

Serves 4–5

NOTE: If using a liquidizer: liquidize all ingredients together except for the oil. Add oil gradually to make a creamy mixture. Add more salt and water if necessary. Then chill.

Onion Soup

METRIC/IMPERIAL

500 g/1 lb onions, thinly sliced
1 tablespoon oil
25 g/1 oz butter
1 level teaspoon salt
1 level teaspoon sugar
1.2 litres/2 pints warm water

1 tablespoon cornflour
1 teaspoon yeast extract
4 x 2.5-cm/1-inch slices
 buttered French bread
1 clove garlic
125 g/4 oz cheese, grated

Cook onions with oil, butter, salt and sugar, over very low heat, covered, stirring occasionally for about 30 minutes until brown.

Pour in water, blended with cornflour and yeast extract. Bring to boil and leave to simmer for 20 minutes.

Toast bread under very low grill and rub with garlic.

Serve soup in a tureen with bread on top and serve cheese in a separate bowl.

Serves 4

VARIATIONS: Sprinkle grated cheese on top of floating bread and brown quickly under grill.

Serve with hot cheese toast, ie grated cheese sprinkled on toast and browned under the grill.

A glass of red dinner wine or sherry can be poured into the soup just before serving.

Leek and Potato Soup

METRIC/IMPERIAL

*500 g/1 lb potatoes, peeled
and sliced*
*500 g/1 lb whole leeks, thinly
sliced*
1.8 litres/3 pints water
1 level tablespoon salt
*25 g/1 oz butter or 2
tablespoons oil*

*½ level tablespoon cornflour
blended with 150 ml/¼ pint
evaporated milk*
*grated nutmeg and pepper to
taste*
*pinch chopped parsley or
chives*

Cook vegetables in salted water with oil until tender. This will take 30 minutes in a covered saucepan, or 5 minutes under pressure (10 minutes in all).

Cool a little, then rub through a strainer with a wooden spoon, or through a vegetable grater or liquidize.

Reheat when needed and stir in cornflour mixture. Boil to thicken. Thin down with water if necessary. Add salt, pepper and nutmeg. Serve in a tureen, garnished with parsley or chives.

Serves 6

VARIATION: Add 125 g/4 oz chopped watercress leaves and stalks when soup is boiling, to thicken. Garnish with roughly chopped watercress leaves instead of parsley or chives.

Vichyssoise

500 g/1 lb white leeks, thinly
  sliced
375 g/12 oz potatoes, peeled
  and thinly sliced
1 clove garlic, sliced
25 g/1 oz butter or margarine
2 litres/3¼ pints water

2 level teaspoons salt
1 level teaspoon glutamate
  powder or brewer's yeast
  powder
150 ml/¼ pint double cream
pepper to taste
pinch chopped chives

Stir leeks, potatoes and garlic with the butter in a saucepan or
in a pressure cooker over low heat for a few minutes. Add
water and salt. Cook for 30 minutes with lid on or for 5
minutes under pressure.

Cool and purée the soup either by rubbing through a
strainer, a vegetable grater or by liquidizing in a blender. Blend
the glutamate powder or yeast with 150 ml/¼ pint water and
stir into the soup. Whisk in the cream. Add pepper and salt, if
needed. (A cold soup needs more salt as a rule.) Chill.

Serve in cups with chives on top.

Serves 6

VARIATION: Prepare 1 packet leek soup (1.1 litres/1¼ pints) and 1 packet
instant potato powder (4 servings) as directed. Mix well together, adding
water to thin to consistency of soup. Then whisk in the cream and continue
as above, but using 275 g/9 oz cream.

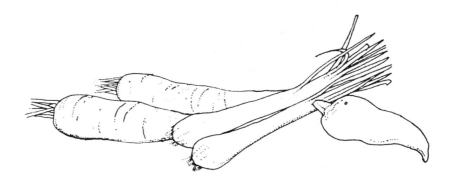

Maltese Soup

METRIC/IMPERIAL

1 medium-sized onion, finely chopped
1 medium-sized carrot, grated coarsely
4 tablespoons vegetable oil
strip lemon rind
1 bay leaf
1 level teaspoon salt
½ level teaspoon pepper
600 ml/1 pint canned tomatoes or 500 g/1 lb skinned and sliced tomatoes

900 ml/1½ pints water
25 g/1 oz butter
25 g/1 oz flour
peel and juice ½ medium-sized orange
sugar to taste
150 ml/¼ pint double cream

Cook onion and carrot in oil over low heat, with lemon rind, bay leaf, salt and pepper in covered pan for 10 minutes. Add tomatoes and water and simmer for 10 minutes longer. Rub through a nylon sieve or liquidize.

Melt butter and flour together, stir in tomato liquid and boil to thicken. Remove from heat.

Cut orange peel into matchsticks, and stir in, with juice. Add sugar to taste, stir in the cream.

Serves 4

37

Lentil and Tomato Soup

METRIC/IMPERIAL

3 tablespoons vegetable oil
1 large onion, chopped
1 carrot, grated coarsely
250 g/8 oz lentils
2 level teaspoons salt
1.8 litres/3 pints water

2 teaspoons mixed herbs
300 ml/½ pint canned or sliced
   fresh tomatoes
2 level tablespoons flour
salt and pepper to taste

In a large saucepan fry together oil, onion, carrot and lentils over low heat for 10 minutes, stirring frequently. Add salt, water and herbs. Bring to boil, simmer until lentils are soft. Add tomatoes and cook for a further 5 minutes.

Rub through a sieve or strainer and return to pan. Stir in flour, blended with a little cold water. Boil to thicken. Add seasonings and more water if soup is too thick. Serve with toast or cubes of bread fried in a little oil.

Serves 5–6

NOTE: The soup has good building value from the mixture of lentils, flour and bread. The lentils are a good source of iron and the tomatoes of vitamin C, if the soup is not kept hot too long.

VARIATION: For Cream of Lentil and Tomato Soup, just before serving whisk in 150 ml/¼ pint evaporated milk or 25 g/1 oz dried milk blended with a little cold water.

Bortsch

METRIC/IMPERIAL

1 large onion, chopped
2 sticks celery
2 tablespoons oil
250 g/8 oz peeled raw
    beetroot, finely grated
900 ml/1½ pints water
2 teaspoons sugar
1 level teaspoon salt

1 level tablespoon cornflour
1 teaspoon yeast extract
1 tablespoon lemon juice
5 tablespoons double or sour
    cream
5 slices lemon
pinch chopped chives

Gently fry onion and celery in oil in a saucepan, stirring often. Add beetroot to pan with water, sugar, salt and yeast extract. Simmer for 20 minutes.

Rub through a strainer or liquidize in a blender. Reheat. Stir in cornflour, blended to thin cream with water. Boil to thicken. Add more salt, if needed. Stir in lemon juice. Pour into bowls and garnish each with 1 tablespoon cream, 1 slice lemon and chives.

Serves 5

VARIATION: Substitute 300 ml/½ pint liquid from sauerkraut or sweet pickled cucumbers for 300 ml/½ pint water in the recipe.

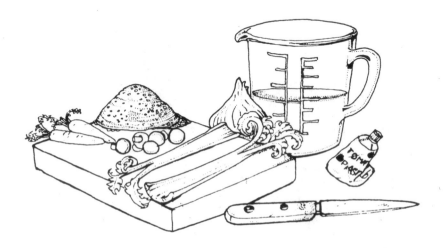

Provençale Soup

METRIC/IMPERIAL

250 g/8 oz potatoes, peeled
and diced
250 g/8 oz carrots, diced
250 g/8 oz leeks or onions
thinly sliced
1 level tablespoon salt
3 litres/5 pints water
250 g/8 oz chopped French
beans or a packet of frozen
cut beans

50 g/2 oz broken spaghetti
1 slice white bread, soaked in
water
1 x 500 g/16 oz can baked
beans
1 level teaspoon pepper
Pistou Sauce (see page 162)

Cook potatoes, carrots and leeks or onions in salted water until tender. This will take 30 minutes in covered saucepan, or 5 minutes under pressure in a pressure cooker, releasing pressure and bringing to boil again.

Stir beans into the boiling soup, then add spaghetti and bread. Cook for 10 minutes. Stir in the baked beans and pepper. Correct the seasoning.

Beat a cupful of soup slowly into the Pistou Sauce. Then transfer to a tureen and pour in the rest of the soup. Serve with hot, toasted slices of French bread.

Serves 6

Minestra

METRIC/IMPERIAL

2–3 tablespoons vegetable oil
1 medium-sized carrot, diced
1 medium-sized onion,
  chopped
1 medium-sized potato, diced
50–75 g/2–3 oz swede, diced
2 stalks celery, chopped
1.5 litres/2½ pints water or
  vegetable stock
1 teaspoon glutamate powder
  or savoury extract
1 tablespoon tomato purée

1 teaspoon mixed herbs
1 teaspoon each sea salt and
  sugar
50 g/2 oz spaghetti
50 g/2 oz French beans
75 g/3 oz sprouts, leeks or
  cabbage, shredded
50 g/2 oz cauliflower sprigs
1 clove garlic, finely chopped
4 tablespoons cooking sherry
little chopped parsley
125 g/4 oz cheese, grated

In a large saucepan heat oil and cook onion, carrot, potato, swede and celery over low heat to develop flavour. Add water, tomato, herbs, salt and sugar. Boil. Add spaghetti and simmer 20 minutes in covered pan.

Add green vegetables, gradually, to keep their colour. Cook 10 minutes. Stir in garlic, parsley and sherry. Serve at once, handing the grated cheese separately in a bowl.

Serves 4–5

NOTE: Allow about 500 g/1 lb mixed vegetables and 50–75 g/2–3 oz pasta to 1.5–1.8 litres/2½–3 pints liquid.

VARIATION: Add a small can of baked beans in tomato sauce just before stirring in the garlic, parsley and sherry.

Rice with Egg and Lemon

METRIC/IMPERIAL

900 ml/1½ pints boiling water
1 level teaspoon salt
1 level teaspoon glutamate
   powder
small piece root ginger, dry or
   fresh
250 g/8 oz rice

2–3 egg yolks
rind and juice of ½ lemon
125 g/4 oz grated dry cheese
   (Parmesan or dry Cheddar)
salt and pepper to taste
pinch nutmeg

To the water, add salt, glutamate powder and root ginger. Sprinkle in rice. Reduce heat. Cover and cook for 15–20 minutes or until the rice is just tender. Remove the ginger.

In a serving casserole or tureen, beat together with a whisk, egg yolks, lemon rind and juice. Add cheese and 2 tablespoons water to make a thick sauce.

Pour in rice and water, stirring well. Add salt, pepper, nutmeg. Serve with French bread or hot buttered toast fingers.

Serves 4

NOTE: To produce chicken flavour, substitute 1 tablespoon Tartex (half a small tin) for glutamate powder, mixing it in with the cheese sauce mixture.

Walnut Soup

METRIC/IMPERIAL

50 g/2 oz walnuts
1 medium-sized onion, finely
  chopped
2 sticks celery, finely chopped
2 tablespoons vegetable oil
25 g/1 oz walnut butter or nut
  fat
25 g/1 oz flour
750 ml/1¼ pints milk and water
1 level teaspoon curry powder

1 level teaspoon salt
½ level teaspoon pepper
2 tablespoons double cream
1 egg yolk
2 tablespoons cold milk
chopped chives or pinch
  paprika

Blanch walnuts 1 minute in boiling water and remove as much brown skin as possible. Mince them, liquidize or put through a nut mill.

Gently fry onion and celery in oil and fat until pale yellow. Add flour, hot milk and water. Stir and cook until thick. Add walnuts, curry powder, salt and pepper. Simmer, covered, for 5–10 minutes.

In a soup tureen or casserole mix cream, yolk and cold milk. Pour in the hot soup. Garnish with chives or paprika. Serve with cubes of fried bread or toast.

Serves 3–4

Nutty Soup

METRIC/IMPERIAL

1 medium-sized onion,
    chopped
2 tablespoons vegetable oil
2 tablespoons tomato purée

50 g/2 oz peanut butter
1 teaspoon yeast extract
600 ml/1 pint hot water
1 teaspoon mixed herbs

Gently fry onion in oil until soft. Add tomato purée, peanut butter, yeast extract, water and herbs. Stir over low heat until thick, for about 5 minutes.

Rub through a nylon strainer, using a wooden spoon. Add salt and pepper to taste. Thin with a little extra water or milk, if liked. Serve with cubes of fried bread or toast.

Serves 3

Garlic Soup

METRIC/IMPERIAL

12 cloves garlic, peeled and
    chopped
1 teaspoon salt
1 level teaspoon black pepper
1.2 litres/2 pints hot water
4 tablespoons olive or
    vegetable oil

1 level teaspoon mixed dried
    herbs or 1 sprig thyme, 4
    sprigs parsley, 1 sage leaf, 1
    bay leaf, tied together with
    thin string
2 egg yolks

Simmer garlic, spices, water, half the oil and the herbs for 30 minutes with lid on. Remove fresh herbs.

Slowly beat remaining oil into the yolks, as for mayonnaise, using a whisk in a basin. Transfer to a tureen.

Beat a cup of hot soup slowly into the egg mixture, then stir in the rest of the hot soup. Serve with toasted, buttered bread, cooked slowly under low grill and with grated cheese.

Serves 4

VARIATION: For a more satisfying soup, add 250 g/8 oz diced potatoes to the pan with the garlic, spices and herbs.

Quick Mixed Vegetable Soup

Metric/Imperial

3 tablespoons oil or 25 g/1 oz
  butter or margarine
1 medium-sized onion, sliced
1 medium-sized carrot,
  chopped
1 medium-sized potato,
  chopped

900 ml/1½ pints boiling water
1 level tablespoon flour (less
  may be needed)
1 level teaspoon salt
1 tablespoon soy sauce or 1
  teaspoon yeast extract

Heat fat and fry vegetables for 1 minute, stirring well. Add water carefully. Bring to boil, then simmer in covered pan for a few minutes. Stir in flour and salt blended with a little cold water. Pour into goblet and liquidize for a few seconds.

Pour back into pan and boil to thicken. Stir in yeast or savoury extract thinned with a little hot water if needed. Season to taste.

Serves 4–5

VARIATION: For Cream of Vegetable Soup, stir 150 ml/¼ pint of evaporated milk into finished soup.

Quick Potato Soup

Metric/Imperial

125 g/4 oz chopped onions or
  leeks fried in fat
125 g/4 oz mashed potato
900 ml/1½ pints water
1 level teaspoon salt

1 level teaspoon nutmeg
1 level tablespoon flour
150 ml/¼ pint evaporated milk

Method as for Quick Mixed Vegetable Soup (see previous recipe).

Serves 4

Quick Bread Soup

METRIC/IMPERIAL

125 g/4 oz onion
125 g/4 oz carrot
2 sticks celery
125 g/4 oz cubed bread
little oil

900 ml/1½ pints water
2 tablespoons tomato purée
1 teaspoon paprika
salt to taste
yeast extract

Fry onion, carrot, celery, and bread in oil. Proceed as for Quick Mixed Vegetable Soup (see page 45). Do not thicken.

Serves 4

Quick Bean and Tomato Soup

METRIC/IMPERIAL

125 g/4 oz chopped onion
125 g/4 oz chopped tomato
little fat
900 ml/1½ pints water
1 x 300 g/10 oz can baked beans

1 teaspoon yeast extract
2 level teaspoons cornflour
chopped parsley to garnish

Method as for Quick Mixed Vegetable Soup (see page 45).

Serves 4

46

Forcemeat Balls   (garnish for soups)

METRIC/IMPERIAL

1 medium-sized onion,
   chopped
2 tablespoons oil
125 g/4 oz sliced bread,
   soaked in water and
   squeezed dry

6 sage leaves, finely chopped
1 egg yolk
salt and pepper to taste

Fry onion in oil until transparent. Mix all ingredients together and shape into marble-sized balls. Fry in butter and oil.

Serves 4–6

VARIATIONS: Use sage and onion packet stuffing. Make up as directed, shape into balls with wet hands and fry as above.

   Use a savoury vegetarian rissole mix. Shape into balls and fry as above.

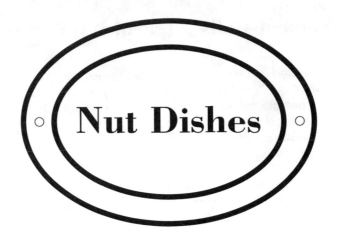

Nut and Rice Rissoles

METRIC/IMPERIAL

125 g/4 oz peanuts, minced or
   125 g/4 oz crunchy peanut
   butter
3 heaped tablespoons boiled
   rice
2 eggs
1 teaspoon yeast extract
1 tablespoon tomato purée
25–50 g/1–2 oz cheese, grated

salt and pepper to taste
6 walnut halves
4–5 tablespoons oil
1 heaped tablespoon flour or
   wheatgerm
few spring onions or chives,
   chopped
Tomato Sauce (see pages
   153–4)

Combine nuts, rice, eggs, yeast extract and tomato with cheese to make a stiff paste. Add salt and pepper to taste.

Shape into balls with wet hands. Coat with brown flour or wheatgerm, by shaking in a paper bag. Flatten to 1-cm/½-inch thickness and press a walnut half on each rissole. Shallow fry in oil to brown both sides.

Serve on a hot dish, sprinkled with spring onion or chives and Tomato Sauce.

Serves 3

Nutty Burgers

METRIC/IMPERIAL

1 medium-sized onion, peeled and chopped

2 tablespoons vegetable oil

1 level tablespoon soup mix (celery or mushroom) or 1 level tablespoon flour

1 level teaspoon salt

2 level teaspoons yeast extract

150 ml/¼ pint water

175 g/6 oz brazil nuts, milled or finely minced

50 g/2 oz cashew nuts, milled or finely minced

125 g/4 oz brown breadcrumbs or 175 g/6 oz moist brown bread, soaked in water then squeezed dry

1 level teaspoon thyme, fresh or dried

2 level tablespoons milk powder or soya flour

1 egg

50 g/2 oz breadcrumbs, rolled oats or coarsely desiccated coconut

4 tablespoons vegetable oil

175 g/6 oz mushrooms, sliced and fried

few tomatoes, halved and grilled or 125 g/4 oz carrots, diced and cooked

little chopped parsley

Fry onions in oil over low heat until pale brown. Stir in flour or soup mix, salt, then yeast extract and water. Boil to make a thick sauce. Remove from heat. Stir in nuts, bread, herbs, milk powder or soya flour and add enough egg to make a moist but firm mixture. Leave to stand, if possible.

With wet hands, shape into four large balls or eight medium-sized ones. Roll in breadcrumbs, oats or coconut and flatten to burger shape.

Fry in hot oil, turning to brown both sides. Then reduce heat and cook 5–7 minutes longer. (Alternatively, bake burgers in a preheated moderate oven at 190°C/375°F, Gas Mark 5, for 30 minutes.)

Arrange on a hot dish with mushrooms and tomatoes or carrots. Sprinkle with parsley.

Serves 4

VARIATION:
Nut Meat Loaf: Put mixture into loaf shape and steam for 1½–2 hours.

Savoury Burgers or Rissoles

METRIC/IMPERIAL

2 medium-sized onions,
peeled and chopped
4 tablespoons vegetable oil
1 level tablespoon soup mix
powder (celery or
mushroom) or 1 level
tablespoon flour
150 ml/¼ pint water
250 g/8 oz fresh peanuts:
125 g/4 oz milled, 125 g/4 oz
minced
125 g/4 oz peanut butter
375 g/12 oz brown
breadcrumbs or 500 g/1 lb
moist bread
2 level teaspoons yeast extract
or 1 level tablespoon
brewer's yeast powder

25 g/1 oz dried skimmed milk
or soya flour
1 level tablespoon fresh
parsley, chopped and mixed
herbs
1 level teaspoon chopped
fresh thyme or 2 teaspoons
mixed herbs
2–3 eggs
salt and pepper to taste
50 g/2 oz dry, grated cheese
mixed with 50 g/2 oz rolled
oats or breadcrumbs
few tomatoes cut in quarters
little chopped parsley or chives
Onion or Tomato Gravy (see
pages 156 and 158)

Fry onion in oil until pale brown. Add soup mix or flour: add water. Stir to a thick sauce. Remove from heat. Add nuts, peanut butter, bread, yeast extract or powder, dried milk or soya flour, herbs and enough eggs to make a moist mix, but firm enough to handle. Add salt and pepper.

With wet hands, shape the mixture into balls about the size of a small orange and roll in the mixture of cheese and oats or breadcrumbs. Flatten to burger shape. Pack into a well-greased baking dish with tomato wedges in between.

Bake on top shelf of a preheated moderately hot oven (200°C/400°F, Gas Mark 6) for 30 minutes or shallow fry in oil for 15 minutes, turning to brown both sides. Drain on paper and keep hot. Serve in baking dish with parsley or chives sprinkled on top, greens, potatoes and Onion or Tomato Gravy.

Serves 6

Nut Roast

METRIC/IMPERIAL

1 medium-sized onion, peeled
and chopped
3 tablespoons vegetable oil
125 g/4 oz tomatoes, skinned
and sliced
25 g/1 oz flour
150 ml/¼ pint water
2 level teaspoons salt
125 g/4 oz hazelnuts, milled or
minced
125 g/4 oz cashew nuts, broken
75-125 g/3–4 oz fresh
breadcrumbs or 150–175 g/
5–6 oz moist bread (soaked,
then squeezed dry)

1 teaspoon mixed, dried herbs
50 g/2 oz cheese, grated or
25 g/1 oz soya flour
2 level teaspoons yeast extract
or soy sauce
1 egg or little water if needed
25 g/1 oz margarine
25 g/1 oz rolled oats

In a saucepan (1.2–1.8-litre/2–3-pint size), gently fry onion in oil, until pale brown. Add tomatoes and cook for 5 minutes. Stir in flour, water and salt. Boil to make a thick sauce. Remove from heat.

Stir in nuts, bread, herbs, cheese or soya flour, yeast extract or soy sauce and mix well, adding more water or egg if needed, to make a fairly stiff mixture. Add more salt and pepper, if needed.

Pack into the bread tin, thickly greased with margarine or nut fat and coated with oats, cornflakes, breadcrumbs or packet stuffing. Cover with greased paper or foil. Bake on middle shelf of preheated moderate oven (180°C/350°F, Gas Mark 4) for about 1 hour.

Serve hot, with gravy or sauce and vegetables, or cold, covered with a savoury glaze.

Serves 4

VARIATION:
Nut Meat Loaf: Steam instead of bake for 1½-2 hours.

Savoury Nut Roast

METRIC/IMPERIAL

*50 g/2 oz walnuts, minced or
    liquidized*

*50 g/2 oz cashew nuts, minced
    or liquidized*

*125 g/4 oz brazil nuts, minced
    or liquidized*

*1 small onion fried in 25 g/1 oz
    butter or oil*

*2 tablespoons wheatgerm if
    liked or 1 level tablespoon
    onion soup mix*

*125 g/4 oz tomatoes, skinned
    and sliced or 150 ml/¼ pint
    canned tomatoes, drained*

2 eggs

*1 level teaspoon mixed herbs
    or thyme*

salt and pepper to taste

Mix all ingredients well together. Pack into greased fireproof dish or tin. Brush top with melted butter or oil. Bake on top shelf of preheated moderate oven (180°C/350°F, Gas Mark 4) until brown.

Serve hot with gravy or onion sauce, greens and potatoes, or cold, sliced with salad, chips or rolls and butter.

Serves 4

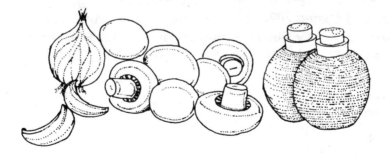

Walnut Roast

METRIC/IMPERIAL

1 medium-sized onion, peeled
and chopped

2–3 tablespoons vegetable oil

25 g/1 oz flour

150 ml/¼ pint tomato juice

1 clove garlic crushed with 1
level teaspoon salt

2 level teaspoons yeast extract
or soy sauce

175 g/6 oz broken walnuts,
milled or minced

50 g/2 oz broken cashew nuts,
milled or minced

75 g/3 oz fresh breadcrumbs,
milled or minced

25 g/1 oz wheatgerm

25 g/1 oz dried milk or soya
flour

1 rounded teaspoon curry
powder

1 rounded teaspoon
marmalade or sweet chutney

1 egg, beaten

175g/6 oz rice, boiled

few lemon slices

50 g/2 oz raw red pepper,
finely chopped, or strips of
canned red pepper

25 g/1 oz margarine or nut fat

25 g/1 oz desiccated coconut

In a saucepan (1.2–1.8-litre/2–3-pint size), gently fry onion in oil, until pale brown. Stir in flour, tomato juice, garlic, salt and yeast extract. Boil to make a thick sauce. Remove from heat.

Stir in nuts, bread, wheatgerm, dried milk or soya flour, curry powder, chutney and enough egg to make a stiff mixture. Add more salt if needed.

Press into loaf tin, greased with margarine or nut fat and coated with desiccated coconut. Cover with greased paper or foil. Bake on middle shelf of a preheated moderate oven (180°C/350°F, Gas Mark 4), for about 1 hour.

Turn out on to a large, hot serving dish. Sprinkle top with paprika, surround with boiled rice and garnish with lemon slices and red pepper.

Serves 4

Grayshott Nut Loaf de Luxe

METRIC/IMPERIAL

1 large onion
2 large tomatoes, skinned
3 large mushrooms
50 g/2 oz butter
1 tablespoon flour
300 ml/½ pint water or
   vegetable stock
1 tablespoon savoury extract
1 rounded teaspoon mixed
   herbs
125 g/4 oz ground almonds

125 g/4 oz ground cashew
   nuts
250 g/8 oz fresh brown
   breadcrumbs
2 eggs
salt and pepper to taste
2 rounded teaspoons agar
   agar
300 ml/½ pint hot water
1 teaspoon yeast extract

Gently fry onion, tomatoes and mushrooms in fat until soft. Stir in flour, stock, savoury extract, herbs and cook for a few minutes. Remove from heat. Mix in nuts, crumbs, eggs and salt and pepper. Let stand for 10 minutes.

Pack into a greased 1-kg/2-lb bread tin and cover with foil or greased paper. Steam for 2 hours.

Serve hot, turned out on an entrée dish, with broccoli, sprouts or cabbage and onion or tomato sauce, or cold, glazed and garnished with parsley or cress, or in overlapping slices with slices of tomato in between.

To glaze: Add agar agar to water, flavoured with yeast extract. Simmer for 5 minutes. Allow to cool a little. Pour and brush evenly and quickly over the cold nutmeat and allow to set.

Serves 8

NOTE: Leftovers can be mashed with nut fat or butter as a spread.

Brown Valencia Savoury

METRIC/IMPERIAL

1 packet sage and onion
  stuffing
175 g/6 oz ground almonds
50 g/2 oz cashew nuts,
  chopped
25 g/1 oz soya flour
2 eggs
15 g/½ oz butter

15 g/½ oz breadcrumbs
Onion Gravy (see page 158)

Make up packet stuffing as directed. Combine stuffing, nuts and soya flour with enough egg to make a moist but firm mixture.

Pack into a thickly buttered 500-g/1-lb loaf tin, coated with breadcrumbs. Cover with foil or greased paper and bake on middle shelf of a preheated moderate oven (180°C/350°F, Gas Mark 4) for about 1 hour, until mixture feels firm, is brown and shrinks a little from sides of tin.

Remove paper or foil and turn out on to a hot dish. Pour a little Onion Gravy round and serve with apple sauce and chipped potatoes.

Serves 4

Groundnut Vegetable Stew

METRIC/IMPERIAL

500 g/1 lb onions, peeled and
  sliced
1 medium-sized red or green
  pepper, seeded
4 tablespoons vegetable oil
500 g/1 lb small aubergines,
  sliced
250 g/8 oz tomatoes, skinned
  and cut into quarters
250 g/8 oz carrots, peeled and
  sliced

2 teaspoons yeast extract
  dissolved in 1.2 litres/2 pints
  hot water
125–175 g/4–6 oz peanut
  butter
125 g/4 oz frozen peas or
  broad beans
1–2 level teaspoons paprika
salt and pepper to taste

Fry onions and pepper in oil over low heat for about 5 minutes. Stir in aubergines, tomatoes, carrots, liquid and peanut butter. Simmer until soft.

Add peas or beans and cook an additional 10 minutes. Season with paprika, salt and pepper. Turn into a hot casserole. Serve with mashed potatoes or rice and a green vegetable.

Serves 6

VARIATIONS: To improve food value, garnish with sliced, hard-boiled eggs.
  Alternatively, stir in 2 tablespoons soya flour and an extra 150 ml/¼ pint water or mix in 150 ml/¼ pint evaporated milk with the seasoning to make a creamy sauce.

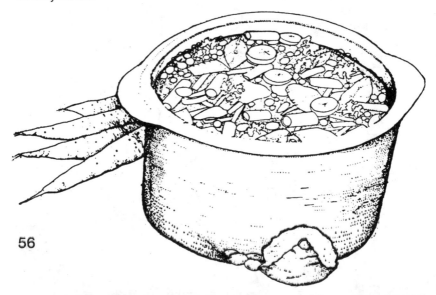

Chestnuts Ury

METRIC/IMPERIAL

*250 g/8 oz dried chestnuts or
500 g/1 lb fresh chestnuts*
*1 medium-sized onion, peeled
and finely chopped*
2–3 tablespoons vegetable oil
25 g/1 oz butter or margarine
*300 ml/½ pint canned
tomatoes or 250 g/8 oz
tomatoes, skinned and
sliced*

2 level teaspoons sugar
1 level teaspoon salt
1 level teaspoon ground ginger
*2 level teaspoons chopped
thyme, fresh or dried or 2
level teaspoons mixed herbs*

Soak chestnuts overnight and steam for 30 minutes over boiling water until just soft or cook in 1.2 litres/2 pints of boiling water.

Gently fry onion in oil and butter or margarine until pale yellow. Add chestnuts and cook 5 minutes longer. Stir in tomatoes, sugar, salt, ginger, thyme or mixed herbs. Cover and cook 15–20 minutes to develop flavour and make a thick, smooth sauce. Pour into a hot serving dish.

Serve with buttered noodles or spaghetti and a salad of diced apple, orange, celery and cress or watercress with lemon vinaigrette dressing.

Serves 4

Creamy Chestnut Savoury

METRIC/IMPERIAL

250 g/8 oz dried chestnuts,
  soaked overnight or 500 g/
  1 lb fresh chestnuts
1 medium-sized onion, finely
  chopped
2 stalks celery, finely chopped
25 g/1 oz butter or margarine
2 level tablespoons flour
300 ml/½ pint cold milk

1 level teaspoon grated
  nutmeg
½ level teaspoon ground
  ginger or fresh root ginger,
  scraped and chopped
1 level teaspoon salt
125 g/4 oz white breadcrumbs
50 g/2 oz Gruyère cheese,
  grated

Steam soaked chestnuts until soft. This will take about 30 minutes. Or slit fresh chestnut skins and steam or boil for 40 minutes. Keep hot whilst peeling.

Gently fry onion and celery in butter or margarine in covered pan until soft. Stir in flour, blended with milk. Boil to thicken. Add chestnuts and seasonings. Simmer for 10 minutes. Stir in half the breadcrumbs to make a thick creamy mixture.

Place in well-buttered shallow ovenproof dish. Top with the remaining crumbs mixed with cheese. Bake on top shelf of a preheated moderate oven (180°C/350°F, Gas Mark 4), for 30–40 minutes until top is brown and crisp.

Serve in the dish with fried mushrooms, tomatoes and green vegetables.

Serves 4

Baked Savoury Nut Pudding

METRIC/IMPERIAL

1 medium-sized onion,
chopped

25 g/1 oz margarine or nut
butter or 2 tablespoons
vegetable oil

500 g/1 lb tomatoes, skinned
and sliced or 600 ml/1 pint
canned tomatoes

1 clove garlic crushed with 1
level teaspoon salt

1 rounded teaspoon dried
herbs or 1 tablespoon fresh
parsley and thyme

little grated lemon rind

250 g/8 oz mashed potato or
mashed potato mix

125–175 g/4–6 oz hazelnuts,
minced or chopped

25 g/1 oz dried milk powder or
50 g/2 oz mild cheese,
grated

little water if needed

Onion Gravy (see page 158)

Fry onion with fat over low heat until pale brown. Add tomatoes, garlic and salt. Cover and cook for 5 minutes. Stir in herbs, lemon, potato, three-quarters of the chopped nuts and milk powder or cheese, to make a soft mixture. Add more water or milk if needed.

Spread mixture in well-greased ovenproof dish, about 3.5 cm/1½ inches thick. Sprinkle remaining nuts on top. Cover with foil or greased paper to keep it moist.

Bake on middle shelf of a preheated moderate oven (180°C/350°F, Gas Mark 4) for 30 minutes. Remove foil or paper and put on top shelf of hot oven (200°C/400°F, Gas Mark 6) for 5 minutes longer to brown.

Serve in the dish, with carrots or cauliflower, a green vegetable and an onion. Serve Onion Gravy separately.

Serves 6

Savoury Almond Pudding

METRIC/IMPERIAL

2 medium-sized onions,
  peeled and chopped
25 g/1 oz butter or margarine
150 ml/¼ pint milk
1 level tablespoon soup mix,
  celery or mushroom
125 g/4 oz almonds, blanched
  and chopped
125 g/4 oz ground almonds
250 g/8 oz white breadcrumbs
1 level teaspoon nutmeg,
  grated

2 level teaspoons salt
pepper to taste
1 level teaspoon ground ginger
  or fresh chopped root ginger
1 egg, beaten
125 g/4 oz cooked peas and
  cooked carrots, diced
few chives, chopped
300 ml/½ pint Creamy Tomato
  Sauce (see page 155)

Cook onion in butter or margarine over low heat until pale yellow. Stir in blended milk and soup mix. Boil to thicken. Cool.

Stir in nuts, breadcrumbs and spices with enough beaten egg and milk to make a soft mixture which drops from the spoon. Add salt and pepper to taste.

Pack into a well-greased 900-ml/1½-pint pudding basin. Cover with foil or greased paper. Steam for 1–1½ hours until firm. Turn out on to a hot dish, sprinkle with chopped chives, surround with Creamy Tomato Sauce and garnish with little heaps of cooked peas and carrots.

Serves 4

Pizzas and Pancakes

Peasant's Pizza

METRIC/IMPERIAL

1 large bread bap, sliced into 4
  rounds
3 cloves garlic, crushed with 1
  level teaspoon salt
75 g/3 oz butter or margarine,
  creamed
2 tablespoons olive oil
250 g/8 oz tomatoes, skinned
and sliced or 300 ml/½ pint
  canned tomatoes, drained
50 g/2 oz spring onions,
  chopped
1 level tablespoon chopped
  parsley
250 g/8 oz cheese, grated

Make garlic butter by mixing garlic and salt with fat.

Toast the bap rounds and spread while hot with garlic butter. Put on a baking sheet and keep hot in the oven.

Mix together oil, tomatoes, onions and parsley.

Put layers of cheese, then tomato mix, on each round, finishing with cheese. Bake on top shelf in a preheated hot oven (200°C/400°F, Gas Mark 6) for 10–15 minutes.

Serves 4

Pizzasaladina

METRIC/IMPERIAL

for bread dough:
150 ml/¼ pint warm water
25 g/1 oz fresh yeast or 5 g/¼
oz (2 teaspoons) dried yeast
1 level teaspoon sugar
375 g/12 oz flour (wholemeal,
plain white or mixed)
1 level teaspoon salt
1 egg

for filling:
250 g/8 oz onions, thinly sliced
2 tablespoons olive or
vegetable oil
1 teaspoon oregano, basil,
marjoram, dried or fresh, or
dried mixed herbs
175 g/6 oz grated cheese
250 g/8 oz tomatoes, sliced
50 g/2 oz stoned black olives

Put water, yeast and sugar in a mixing bowl. If using dried yeast, leave for 5 minutes to soften. Add all at once the flour, salt and egg. Mix with one hand and add more water if needed, until no dry flour is left in the bowl.

Make a soft dough by squeezing and working with the hand. Shape to a ball and put in an oiled saucepan with lid, or inside an oiled polythene bag. Leave to rise and double its original size. This will take 30–45 minutes.

Fry onions very slowly with oil and herbs in a thick covered saucepan until transparent. This should take about 30 minutes.

Divide risen dough into four or five pieces on an oiled board or table. Shape each dough piece to a ball and roll out to a 15-cm/6-inch round, 2.5 mm/⅛ inch thick. Leave for 2 or 3 minutes. Fit each round into an oiled sandwich tin.

Cover each round with layers of onions and oil, cheese, tomatoes and herbs, finishing with a layer of cheese. Arrange olives on top. Leave to stand for 15–45 minutes. Bake on top shelf of a preheated hot oven (200°C/400°F, Gas Mark 6) for 25 minutes.

Serves 4

Pizzaladiere Niçoise

METRIC/IMPERIAL

risen bread dough (see
  Pizzasaladina opposite)
500 g/1 lb onions, thinly sliced
3 tablespoons olive oil
2 cloves garlic, crushed with
  1 level teaspoon salt

½ level teaspoon freshly
  ground black pepper
125 g/4 oz black olives, stoned
175 g/6 oz cheese, grated

Fry onions very slowly with oil, garlic and salt in a thick covered pan until transparent. Season with pepper. Remove from heat and mix in the cheese.

Roll out risen bread dough 2.5 mm/⅛ inch thick, on a board or table, either brushed with oil or lightly floured. Leave 2–3 minutes.

Lay the sheet of dough over an oiled Swiss roll tin. Trim off surplus dough, squeeze to a ball and roll again. Cut thin strips, 5 mm/¼ inch wide, with a sharp knife.

Put in cheese and onion filling. Arrange dough strips in a lattice over the top and place an olive in each square. Brush the dough strips with oil. Leave the pizza for 15 minutes. Bake on top shelf, in a preheated hot oven (200°C/400°F, Gas Mark 6) for 15–20 minutes.

Serves 4

VARIATIONS: Try using different cheeses and herbs, such as chopped fresh sage with grated Lancashire cheese and lightly fried onion.

Alternatively, combine fried onions and mushrooms, season with a pinch of ground ginger, top with a mixture of cottage cheese and grated Cheddar cheese and garnish with chopped chives or parsley.

Pancakes

METRIC/IMPERIAL
75–125 g/3–4 oz plain flour
150–300 ml/¼–½ pint milk
1 or 2 eggs, beaten
1 tablespoon oil

Put flour in a mixing bowl and stir in enough milk to make a smooth, thick paste. Stir in 1 egg and another egg or more milk, if necessary, to make a pouring cream.

Heat oil in a thick pan until it runs. Pour in just enough batter to cover the pan, tilting as you pour. Reduce heat. Turn when bubbles appear and brown the other side. Slide off on to kitchen paper and repeat for next pancake. Keep hot on a dish, with a square of greaseproof paper between each pancake.

Serves 4

NOTE: Pancake batter can be stored in a refrigerator for three days. Pancakes, layered with greaseproof paper and stored in a polythene bag, will keep for three or four days in a cold place.

VARIATIONS:
Richer batter: Use 2 eggs and less milk.
Lighter batter: Mix in yolks first, then fold in stiffly beaten whites.
Cheaper batter: Mix in 1 teaspoon dried yeast or 5 g/¼ oz fresh yeast with the batter and omit the egg. Stand in warm place for 10 minutes. Or mix in 1 rounded tablespoon soya flour and omit the egg and the milk, using water to mix.

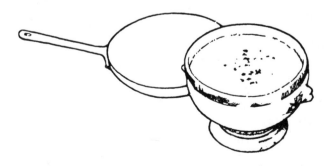

Stuffed Pancakes

METRIC/IMPERIAL

Pancakes (see opposite)
1 x 300 g/10 oz can baked
   beans in tomato sauce
350 g/8 oz cheese, grated

300 ml/½ pint tomato juice
50 g/2 oz butter or margarine,
   melted

Make pancakes and keep hot.

Mash beans and sauce with half the cheese to a smooth paste. Place a spoonful of filling in middle of each cooked pancake and fold over.

Place rolled pancakes side by side in ovenproof dish. Pour over tomato juice and melted butter. Sprinkle with remaining cheese.

Bake on top shelf of a preheated moderately hot oven (190°C/375°F, Gas Mark 5) for about 15 minutes, until browned and bubbling hot.

Serves 4

OTHER FILLINGS:

Cheese and Tomato Filling: Beat the following ingredients to a soft paste: 125 g/4 oz cottage cheese; 25 g/1 oz softened butter; 2 teaspoons onion soup mix; and 2 teaspoons tomato purée.

Swiss Cheese Filling: Mix together until soft: 125 g/4 oz Gruyère cheese; 2 tablespoons double cream; 2 tablespoons white breadcrumbs; 50 g/2 oz finely chopped raw celery; and 25 g/1 oz walnuts.

Stacked Savoury Pancakes

METRIC/IMPERIAL

Pancakes (see page 64)
250 g/8 oz onion, thinly sliced
4 tablespoons vegetable oil

500 g/1 lb tomatoes, skinned
and thinly sliced
250 g/8 oz cheese, grated

Make pancakes and keep hot.

Fry onion in oil until golden over low heat. Pile up pancakes with a thin layer of fried onion, sliced tomato and cheese between each pancake. Arrange surplus tomatoes round the pile and top with cheese.

Bake on top shelf of a preheated moderately hot oven (190°C/375°F, Gas Mark 5), until top is brown and liquid is bubbling. To serve, cut in wedges or lift off each pancake.

Serve with salad, green vegetables or peas and carrots.

Serves 4

Breadcrumb Pancakes

METRIC/IMPERIAL

50 g/2 oz plain flour
50 g/2 oz white or brown
breadcrumbs
2 eggs, beaten

2 teaspoons baking powder
150 ml/¼ pint milk
1 teaspoon salt
2 tablespoons oil

Collect all ingredients except oil in a large bowl and mix to a pouring batter.

Heat oil in a large frying pan and pour in enough batter to make 10-cm/4-inch round pancakes. Turn when bubbles appear and brown on other side.

Serve with hot baked beans in tomato sauce and grated cheese.

Serves 4

Blinis

Metric/Imperial

for pancakes:
200-250 g/7–8 oz flour
300 ml/½ pint boiled, cooled
    milk or reconstituted dried
    milk or canned milk
1 teaspoon sugar
1 egg yolk
15 g/½ oz fresh yeast or 2 level
    teaspoons dried yeast
1 teaspoon oil

for filling:
125 g/4 oz mushrooms,
    chopped
25 g/1 oz butter
1 small can condensed
    mushroom soup
50 g/2 oz cheese, grated

Put flour, milk, sugar, egg yolk and yeast in a bowl. Mix to a batter with wooden spoon. Leave in a warm place for 10 minutes.

Add a little more milk or water to make a pouring batter. Fold in the stiffly beaten whites.

Pour oil into hot pan. Pour in batter to just cover bottom of pan. Turn when brown.

Stack pancakes with squares of greaseproof paper in between and keep hot.

Fry mushrooms in butter. Stir in condensed soup and add enough cheese to make a soft paste. Put a spoonful of filling on each pancake and fold over. Arrange on a dish. Sprinkle with remaining cheese and brown under grill. Serve with green salad.

Serves 4

Variation: Stir in 50 g/2 oz milled cashew nuts instead of cheese.

Croûton Pancake

METRIC/IMPERIAL

60 cubes French bread
2 tablespoons vegetable oil
40 g/1½ oz butter
2 eggs
150 ml/¼ pint milk

50–75 g/2–3 oz Gruyère
  cheese, grated
salt and pepper to taste
few grilled tomatoes
few sprigs watercress

Fry bread cubes in oil and butter until pale brown.

In large bowl beat eggs, milk, cheese and seasonings with a fork. Pour egg mixture over croûtons in frying pan. Cover. Cook without stirring for 10 minutes over lowest possible heat. Slide the pancake out on to a platter. Garnish with tomatoes and watercress.

Serves 2–3

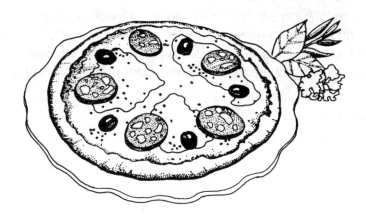

68

Pasta

Spaghetti Salad

METRIC/IMPERIAL

250 g/8 oz spaghetti
750 ml/1¼ pints boiling, salted
  water
2 tablespoons soy, corn or nut
  oil
1 tablespoon light soy sauce or
  1 teaspoon Worcestershire
  sauce

2 spring onions, finely
  chopped
2 sticks celery
50 g/2 oz red pepper
150 g/5 oz bean sprouts
  (optional)
salt and pepper to taste

Boil spaghetti until just tender. Rinse under cold tap. Drain
well and chill. Stir in oil, soy or Worcestershire sauce, onion,
celery, pepper and bean sprouts. Season.

Serves 4

VARIATION: Use mayonnaise instead of oil.

Spaghetti Lyonnaise au Gratin

METRIC/IMPERIAL

900 ml/1½ pints salted water
250 g/8 oz spaghetti, broken
2–3 medium-sized onions,
* chopped*
2 tablespoons vegetable oil
2 teaspoons cornflour
½ teaspoon nutmeg, grated
½ teaspoon pepper

2 tablespoons cold water
150 ml/¼ pint evaporated milk
75–125 g/3–4 oz cheese,
* grated*
2–3 tablespoons wheatgerm or
* rolled oats*
little chopped parsley or chives

Bring water to fast boil. Slowly drop in the spaghetti. After 5 minutes, add the onion and vegetable oil, and continue to boil.

Blend cornflour, nutmeg and pepper with water, then milk, in a bowl.

When spaghetti is just soft, stir in the separate liquid mixture. Boil 1 minute to thicken. Season to taste. Pour into shallow fireproof dish.

Top with mixture of cheese and wheatgerm or oats. Brown under grill. Garnish with parsley or chives. Serve with broccoli, kale, or sprouts or with a salad of chicory, sliced tomato and orange, with French dressing.

Serves 4–5

NOTE: For stronger flavour cook onion slowly in fat until transparent.

Spaghetti with Green Garlic Sauce

METRIC/IMPERIAL

Pesto Sauce (see page 30)
900 ml/1½ pints boiling, salted
water

250 g/8 oz noodles or
spaghetti
25 g/1 oz butter

Drop the pasta slowly into boiling water. Cook until just soft. Drain in a colander and wash under hot tap. Return to pan and mix in butter.

Serve piled in a big dish and pour the green garlic sauce over the top. Mix at the table and hand a bowl of grated cheese separately.

Serves 4–5

VARIATION: Fill a large ovenproof dish with layers of cooked spaghetti, some garlic sauce and grated cheese, finishing with cheese on top. Bake in a hot oven 15 minutes.

Spaghetti Africaine

METRIC/IMPERIAL

250 g/8 oz spaghetti or
noodles
750 ml/1¼ pints boiling, salted
water
1 onion, chopped
2 tablespoons oil
2 teaspoons curry powder
150 ml/¼ pint tomato juice

1 teaspoon yeast extract
3 tablespoons peanut butter
50 g/2 oz sultanas
rind and juice of ½ lemon
few salted peanuts
few sprigs watercress
few lemon twists

Boil spaghetti until just tender. Drain.

Fry onion in oil until light brown. Stir in curry powder, tomato juice, yeast extract, peanut butter, sultanas, lemon rind and juice, to make a smooth sauce. Stir in the spaghetti and heat through. Serve piled on dish, garnished with peanuts, watercress, and lemon twists.

Serves 3

Spaghetti Campania

METRIC/IMPERIAL

4 tablespoons olive oil

125 g/4 oz onion, finely chopped

125 g/4 oz carrot, grated

125 g/4 oz green pepper, seeded and finely chopped

1 clove garlic, crushed with ½ level teaspoon salt

250 g/8 oz spaghetti or other pasta

900 ml/1½ pints boiling, salted water

15 g/½ oz butter or 1 tablespoon oil

150 ml/¼ pint tomato purée (150 g/5 oz)

150 ml/¼ pint water

1 rounded teaspoon sugar

1 rounded teaspoon each of thyme and marjoram, chopped or 1 level teaspoon dried herbs

salt and pepper to taste

few black olives or pickled walnuts, cut in quarters

Fry in oil over low heat, onion, carrot, pepper and garlic for 10 minutes.

Drop pasta slowly into boiling water. Cook until just soft, drain in a colander and wash under hot tap. Return to pan with butter or oil. Keep hot.

While pasta is cooking, continue making the sauce. Add tomato, water, sugar and herbs. Simmer for 20 minutes until thick and smooth. Season.

Serve the spaghetti piled up on a hot dish, garnished with black olives or pickled walnuts with the vegetable sauce spooned round.

Serves 4

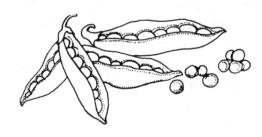

Macaroni with Peas

METRIC/IMPERIAL

*250 g/8 oz macaroni,
preferably shell macaroni*
*900 ml/1½ pints boiling, salted
water*
*1 large carrot, peeled and
diced small*
125 g/4 oz fresh or frozen peas
*2–3 tablespoons vegetable oil
or 25 g/1 oz butter*

*1 medium-sized onion, finely
chopped*
4 tablespoons evaporated milk
125 g/4 oz cheese, cubed
salt and pepper to taste
*strips of canned red pepper or
finely chopped fresh pepper*

Drop macaroni slowly into water, so that boiling does not
stop. Boil for 5 minutes. Add carrot. Boil 5 minutes longer.
Add peas. Boil all together an additional 5 minutes.

Stir in the oil or butter and onion. Cook with lid off to
evaporate most of the water. The vegetables and macaroni
should be just soft.

Remove from heat, stir in milk and cheese, and season.
Serve piled up in hot casserole or dish, garnished with red
peppers.

Serves 4

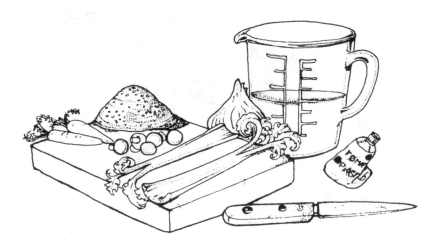

Macaroni with Cheese and Tomatoes

METRIC/IMPERIAL

*250 g/8 oz macaroni or
spaghetti*
*1.2 litres/2 pints boiling, salted
water*
*2 tablespoons oil or 25 g/1 oz
butter*
*175–250 g/6–8 oz tomatoes
skinned and sliced or 300
ml/½ pint canned tomatoes*

1 rounded teaspoon sugar
*1 rounded teaspoon mixed
herbs, dry or fresh*
175 g/6 oz cheese, grated
*2 rounded teaspoons brewer's
yeast powder or onion soup
mix*
little chopped parsley or chives

Drop macaroni or spaghetti slowly into water, so that boiling does not stop. Cook until soft. Strain off water. Stir in oil, tomatoes, sugar and herbs and heat through.

Remove from heat, stir in cheese and yeast or soup mix. Serve piled up on a hot dish, garnished with parsley or chives.

Serves 4

Egg Noodles

METRIC/IMPERIAL

3 eggs, beaten
1 tablespoon oil
2 level teaspoons salt

500 g/1 lb plain flour
boiling, salted water
little oil or margarine

Put eggs, oil and salt into centre of flour in a bowl and mix by hand to stiff, firm dough. Add cold water as needed. Work the dough, until it is smooth and elastic, for about 5–10 minutes.

Divide into four portions and roll out each piece as thinly as possible on a lightly floured board or table top. Leave for 2–3 minutes. Roll up loosely and cut into strips, about 5 mm/¼ inch wide, with a sharp knife.

Dry the noodles by spreading the strips on tea towels or by draping them over a line of string in a warm, airy kitchen. They will be dry enough to use in about 1 hour.

Drop slowly into large saucepan, half-filled with boiling, salted water, so that boiling does not stop. Cook uncovered for about 7 minutes. Fully dried noodles will take 10–15 minutes. Put in a colander, wash under hot tap and drain. Keep hot in covered saucepan. Mix in oil or margarine to prevent noodles from sticking together.

Serves 6

VARIATION:
Tomato Noodles: Add a packet tomato soup mix to the bowl of flour and proceed as above.

Noodles with Buttered Almonds

METRIC/IMPERIAL
250 g/8 oz noodles
1.2 litres/2 pints boiling, salted
    water
125 g/4 oz split, blanched
    almonds

125 g/4 oz unsalted butter
salt, pepper and nutmeg to
    taste
few sprigs watercress
few lemon twists

Cook the noodles as in recipe on page 75. Drain and keep hot.

Cook almonds in half the butter over a low heat until golden. Add the rest of the butter and cook until foamy. Remove from heat. Stir in noodles. Season. Turn into a hot serving dish and garnish with watercress and lemon twists.

Serves 4

VARIATION:
Noodles with Buttered Crumbs: Substitute 50 g/2 oz brown or white breadcrumbs for almonds, cooking them in the butter in the same way. Remove from heat. Pour butter and crumbs over noodles and serve immediately.

Soya Noodles

METRIC/IMPERIAL
500 g/1 lb plain flour
50 g/2 oz soya flour
1 tablespoon oil

3 level teaspoons salt
boiling, salted water

Measure flour, oil and salt into a bowl. Slowly add enough water to make a firm dough which leaves bowl and fingers clean. Work well in the bowl, until the dough is smooth and elastic. Divide into four portions.

Proceed as in recipe for Egg Noodles (see page 75).

Serves 8

Noodles al Sugo

METRIC/IMPERIAL

750 g/1½ lb fresh tomatoes or
   750 ml/1¼ pints canned
   tomatoes
1 level teaspoon salt
½ level teaspoon pepper
2 level teaspoons sugar
1 bay leaf
375 g/12 oz noodles

1.8 litres/3 pints boiling, salted
   water
2 tablespoons olive oil
large sprig fresh or 1 teaspoon
   dried marjoram or thyme
little chopped chives or parsley
125–175 g/4–6 oz grated
   cheese

Cook tomatoes in thick covered pan with salt, pepper, sugar and bay leaf very slowly for about 1 hour. Liquidize or rub through a nylon sieve.

Drop noodles slowly into large saucepan of boiling, salted water. Cook 10 minutes and drain through a colander.

Heat tomato pulp in a pan, with oil and marjoram.

Stir in noodles. Serve in a hot dish, garnished with chives or parsley.

Hand grated cheese separately.

Serves 4

Green Noodle Pasta

METRIC/IMPERIAL

250 g/8 oz spinach or
  150 ml/¼ pint spinach purée
3 tablespoons boiling water
500 g/1 lb plain flour
2 level teaspoons salt
2 tablespoons oil
2 eggs, beaten

boiling, salted water
250–375 g/8–12 oz Bel Paese
  cheese, diced
250 g/8 oz tomatoes, skinned,
  sliced and fried in 2
  tablespoons oil or red and
  green peppers, sliced

Cook spinach with water over strong heat to keep the fresh green colour. Press the spinach down with a wooden spoon. Cook for 5 minutes. Cool. Liquidize in an electric blender or rub through a wire sieve or strainer.

Mix together flour, salt, half the oil, eggs and spinach purée to make a stiff dough which leaves bowl clean. Squeeze and work the dough with one hand until it feels firm. Divide into four portions. Proceed as in recipe for Egg Noodles (see page 75).

Keep noodles hot in a saucepan, using remaining oil to keep them from sticking together. Add cheese. Turn out into a hot serving dish and garnish with tomatoes or red and green peppers.

Serves 6

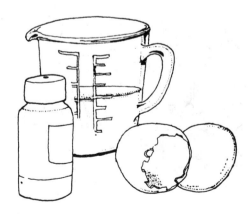

Three-Flavoured Noodles

METRIC/IMPERIAL

250 g/8 oz noodles
1.2 litres/2 pints boiling, salted water
4 tablespoons Tomato Sauce (see pages 153–4)
salt and pepper to taste
1 teaspoon sugar
1 teaspoon glutamate powder
3 tablespoons curry powder
1 tablespoon vegetable oil

1 medium-sized onion, sliced into thin rings
50 g/2 oz cashew nuts, crushed or 50 g/2 oz cashew nut cream
4 tablespoons water
1 large tomato, cut into wedges
little chopped parsley or cress

Boil noodles until just done. Rinse in a colander first under cold water, then under hot. Drain. Keep hot in serving dish.

Mix together sauce, seasonings and glutamate powder.

Gently fry curry powder in oil. Add onion and fry 1 minute longer. Stir in nuts, water, sauce and tomato. Pour sauce over noodles or stir noodles into sauce. Pile on dish. Garnish with parsley or cress.

Serves 3

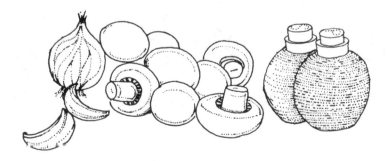

79

Noodles with Cheese

METRIC/IMPERIAL

500 g/1 lb noodles, dry or fresh
boiling, salted water
375 g/12 oz tomatoes, skinned
and sliced or 300 ml/½ pint
canned tomatoes
50 g/2 oz butter or 4
tablespoons olive or
vegetable oil

1 clove garlic, crushed with ½
teaspoon salt
250–375 g/8–12 oz cheese,
grated
2 heaped teaspoons brewer's
yeast powder (optional)
little chopped chives or parsley
few black olives

Drop the noodles slowly into large saucepan, half filled with boiling, salted water, so that the boiling does not stop. Cook 7–10 minutes, until just tender.

Drain off water. Stir in tomatoes, oil or butter and garlic. Heat through again. Remove from heat. Stir in cheese, mixed with yeast powder.

Serve piled up on a hot dish, garnished with chives or parsley and olives.

Serves 5

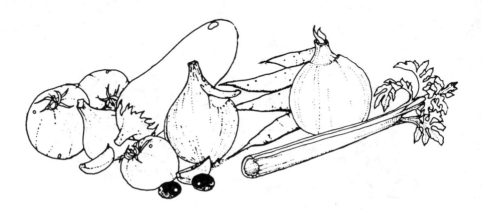

Nutty Pasta

METRIC/IMPERIAL

250 g/8 oz noodles or spaghetti
1.2 litres/2 pints boiling, salted
   water
1 onion, finely chopped
2 tablespoons vegetable oil
150 ml/¼ pint tomato juice
3 tablespoons crunchy peanut
   butter

1 teaspoon yeast extract or
   soy sauce
few red and green peppers,
   thinly sliced and lightly fried
   in 1 tablespoon oil
few salted peanuts
few lemon twists

Boil noodles or spaghetti until just tender. Drain.

Fry onion in oil until golden brown. Stir in tomato juice, peanut butter, yeast extract or soy sauce and more tomato juice, if needed, to make a smooth sauce. Stir in noodles and heat through. Serve on a hot dish garnished with sliced peppers, peanuts and lemon twists.

Serves 3

Pasta with Cream Cheese and Walnuts

METRIC/IMPERIAL

250 g/8 oz pasta shells
1.2 litres/2 pints boiling, salted
   water
25 g/1 oz unsalted butter
175–250 g/6–8 oz double
   cream cheese or 125 g/4 oz
   cottage cheese and 150
   ml/¼ pint double cream

2 tablespoons grated dry
   cheese
50–75 g/2–3 oz walnuts,
   roughly chopped
pinch curry powder

Drop pasta shells gradually into boiling water. Simmer in open saucepan until soft. Drain well. Keep hot.

Melt butter and cream cheese in ovenproof dish over low heat. Stir in the pasta, dry cheese, walnuts and curry powder. Serve with a green salad.

Serves 4

Pasta Hotpot

METRIC/IMPERIAL

125 g/4 oz pasta or spaghetti
600 ml/1 pint boiling, salted
  water
125 g/4 oz marrow, diced
4 sticks celery, cut in 1-cm/
  ½-inch slices
125 g/4 oz carrot, thinly sliced
25 g/1 oz butter
4–6 tablespoons evaporated
  milk

1 x 300 g/10 oz can sweetcorn
1 teaspoon fresh ginger, finely
  chopped or ½ teaspoon
  ground ginger mixed with 1
  teaspoon sugar
salt and pepper to taste
4 spring onions, chopped
2 tablespoons oil
125 g/4 oz cheese, grated

Drop the spaghetti into boiling water in a 1.8-litre/3-pint saucepan. Cook for 5 minutes. Add marrow, celery, carrot and butter. Bring to the boil and cook for 10 minutes longer. Stir in milk, sweetcorn and ginger. Season.

Gently cook onion in oil for a few minutes until a rich green colour.

Serve pasta in a casserole, with onions on top. Hand round a dish of grated cheese separately.

Serves 3

NOTE: A mixture of onions and chopped chives can be used instead of spring onions.

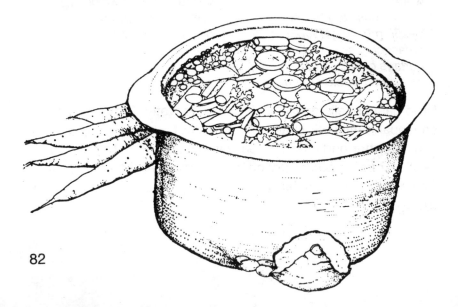

Ravioli

METRIC/IMPERIAL

noodle pasta (see recipe for Egg Noodles, page 75), using 250 g/8 oz plain flour

boiling, salted water little oil or butter

Divide the noodle paste into two and roll each piece out very thinly on a floured board or table. Let stand for 5 minutes.

On one sheet of pasta, put a teaspoonful of filling every 5 cm/2 inches and brush round with water. Cover with the second sheet of pasta and press it gently round each little heap of filling.

Using a sharp knife or a wooden pastry wheel, cut the dough into 5-cm/2-inch squares, making sure the edges are firmly sealed round the filling. Dry ravioli on a cake rack or on a clean tea towel or sheets of kitchen paper for about 1 hour.

Drop the ravioli slowly into a large saucepan of rapidly boiling, salted water. Cook for 6–10 minutes. Drain in a colander. Return ravioli to the pan and shake with a little oil or butter. Serve with sauce and/or garnish.

Serves 4–5

NOTE: Trimmings of pasta left over can be kneaded together, rolled out and used to make noodles.

Ravioli Fillings

Cheese and Tomato:

METRIC/IMPERIAL

250 g/8 oz cheese, grated
2 level teaspoons yeast extract

1 level teaspoon mixed herbs
3–4 tablespoons tomato purée

Mix all ingredients together. Add a little water to make a stiff paste.

Serves 4–5

Mushroom:

METRIC/IMPERIAL
1 medium-sized onion,
  chopped
250 g/8 oz mushrooms,
  chopped
50 g/2 oz butter
½ teaspoon ground ginger

1 teaspoon salt
½ teaspoon pepper
1 teaspoon glutamate powder
  (optional)
2 tablespoons dried milk
  powder or ground almonds

Fry onion and mushrooms in fat over low heat with ginger, salt, pepper and glutamate powder. When soft, remove from heat, mash well with wooden spoon and work in enough powder or almonds to make a soft paste.

Serves 4–5

Baked Beans and Cheese:

METRIC/IMPERIAL
1 x 300 g/10 oz can baked
  beans in tomato sauce
25 g/1 oz butter or margarine,
  softened

4 level teaspoons onion soup
  powder or yeast powder
250 g/8 oz strong Cheddar
  cheese, grated

Mash beans and sauce with margarine and soup powder. Work in enough grated cheese to make a stiff paste.

Serves 4–5

Savoury Nut:

METRIC/IMPERIAL
125–175 g/4–6 oz canned nut
  mixture
125 g/4 oz cottage cheese

25 g/1 oz butter or margarine,
  softened

Make up nut mixture as directed on tin. Combine cottage cheese and butter or margarine, and work in enough nut mixture to make a stiff paste.

Serves 4–5

Savoury Soya:

METRIC/IMPERIAL

1 medium-sized onion, finely
   chopped
50 g/2 oz butter or margarine
1 level tablespoon celery or
   leek soup mix

300 ml/½ pint tomato juice
250 g/8 oz soya flour
3 teaspoons yeast extract
125 g/4 oz fresh breadcrumbs
2 eggs, beaten

Lightly fry onion in butter. Mix in next four ingredients. Cook until almost dry, stirring well. Cool a little and stir in egg.

Serves 8–10

NOTE: Surplus filling will keep, if wrapped in foil and stored in refrigerator.

Nut Meat:

METRIC/IMPERIAL

1 can nut meat
little yeast extract
1–2 teaspoons onion, celery,
   leek or mushroom soup
   powder

Combine all ingredients together.

Serves 4

Tasty:

METRIC/IMPERIAL

125 g/4 oz Tartex
50 g/2 oz ground almonds
1–2 teaspoons chopped
   parsley

1–2 teaspoons chopped thyme
50 g/2 oz cottage cheese

Combine to make a soft paste.

Serves 4–5

Ravioli, Russian-Style

METRIC/IMPERIAL

for dough:
1 level teaspoon dried yeast or
  5 g/¼ oz fresh yeast
2 tablespoons warm water
pinch sugar
125 g/4 oz flour
1 level teaspoon salt
1 egg
25 g/1 oz butter or margarine
  or 2 tablespoons oil

for filling:
50 g/2 oz mushrooms, chopped
1 small onion, finely chopped
2 tablespoons oil or 25 g/1 oz
  nut fat
3 tablespoons boiled rice
1 hard-boiled egg, chopped
salt and pepper to taste
2 teaspoons savoury or yeast
  extract or 25 g/1 oz Tartex

Mix together in large bowl, yeast, water and sugar. Let stand 5 minutes. Add flour, salt and egg. Mix to a soft dough with wooden spoon or with the hand. Add a little more flour or water if needed. Squeeze and work the soft dough with the hands for a few minutes. Then work in fat.

Place bowl inside a polythene bag or press a square of polythene on top of the dough and leave on the table for 30–40 minutes to rise double.

Cook chopped mushrooms and onion in oil over low heat for about 5 minutes. Remove from heat. Stir in rice, egg and seasonings.

Flatten dough with the hands on lightly floured board. Roll up loosely to resemble Swiss roll. Put dough in polythene bag and chill. Leave for 5 minutes. Roll out dough thinly. Cut into 5-cm/2-inch rounds with pastry cutter. Put a teaspoon of filling on each. Wet edges half-way round, fold over, press edges together firmly, pinch to decorate. Place on oiled paper on a cake rack. Cover with polythene. Leave for 15 minutes.

Drop into hot oil at 190°C/380°F, one by one, and remove with perforated spoon when brown. Or place on greased baking sheet and brush with egg. Bake on top shelf of a preheated hot oven (200°C/400°F, Gas Mark 6) for 15 minutes. Drain. Serve.

Serves 4

Hungarian Gnocchi

METRIC/IMPERIAL

125 g/4 oz flour
75 g/3 oz butter, 25 g/1 oz
  melted
300 ml/½ pint hot milk
½ level teaspoon salt
¼ level teaspoon nutmeg

3 eggs
boiling, salted water
little oil
125–175 g/4–6 oz cheese,
  grated

Cook flour and 50 g/2 oz butter together over low heat for 3 minutes, stirring with wooden spoon. Add hot milk and seasonings and beat to a smooth mixture. Remove from heat and beat in eggs. The mixture should leave sides of pan clean. Cool a little.

Put in a forcing bag with 1-cm/½-inch plain nozzle. Pipe small pieces into boiling water. Remove with perforated spoon when they rise to the surface. Dry.

Place the gnocchi in an oiled ovenproof dish. Cover with grated cheese and melted butter. Brown under grill.

Serves 4

NOTE: The choux paste could be moulded into balls with wet hands, instead of using a forcing bag.

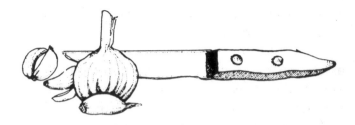

87

Potato Dumplings

METRIC/IMPERIAL

for sauce:

1 teaspoon mixed herbs
4 parsley stalks
2 rounded tablespoons finely
   chopped onion
2 rounded tablespoons
   coarsely grated carrot
25 g/1 oz butter
1 tablespoon tomato purée
450 ml/¾ pint water
1 level teaspoon yeast extract
2 level teaspoons cornflour
salt and pepper to taste

for dumplings:

500 g/1 lb potatoes, boiled or
   steamed
75 g/3 oz plain flour
2 eggs, separated
salt and pepper to taste
50 g/2 oz butter
900 ml/1 ½ pints gently boiling,
   salted water
175 g/6 oz cheese, grated

Cook herbs and vegetables in butter over low heat for 10 minutes. Add purée, water and yeast extract. Simmer. Press through a strainer. Return to pan. Stir in cornflour, blended with a little water. Boil to thicken. Season. Reheat sauce as required.

Rub hot potatoes through a wire sieve or vegetable grater, into a bowl. Mix in flour, 1 egg and 1 egg yolk and butter. Season. Roll into walnut-sized balls or small sausage shapes. Drop one by one into boiling water. Cook 10 minutes. Remove with perforated spoon. Drain.

Serve on a hot dish with sauce poured over, sprinkled with a little cheese. Hand rest of cheese separately.

Serves 4

Gnocchi Romana

METRIC/IMPERIAL

125 g/4 oz fine or coarse
  semolina
600 ml/1 pint boiling, salted
  water
75 g/3 oz butter or margarine
125 g/4 oz cheese, grated
2 eggs, beaten

2 teaspoons brewer's yeast
  powder
2 heaped tablespoons dried
  skimmed milk
pinch grated nutmeg
pepper to taste
few sprigs watercress

Sprinkle semolina slowly into liquid. Stir and cook over low heat until thick and smooth. Remove from heat.

Stir in 25 g/1 oz each butter and cheese, the eggs, brewer's yeast powder, milk powder, nutmeg and pepper. Mix thoroughly. Pour onto a large dish, so that the mixture is about 1 cm/½ inch thick. Allow to cool.

When cold, shape into 2.5-cm/1-inch squares, or walnut-sized balls or small rounds, using smallest pastry cutter.

Put gnocchi into an oiled, shallow baking dish. Sprinkle with remaining grated cheese and melted butter. Brown under the grill or bake on top shelf of a preheated moderate oven (180°C/350°F, Gas Mark 4) for about 15 minutes.

Serve garnished with watercress.

Serves 3–4

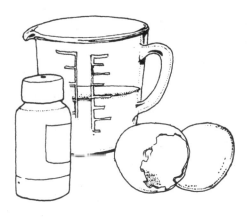

Tarhonya

METRIC/IMPERIAL

375 g/12 oz plain flour, white
or brown
1 egg yolk

1 level teaspoon salt
150 ml/¼ pint yogurt

Mix flour, egg yolk and salt with enough yogurt to make a stiff dough. Squeeze and work the dough well for 2–3 minutes. Roll out thinly on floured board. Leave 5 minutes. Roll up loosely to resemble Swiss roll. Cut into 5-mm/¼-inch slices as for noodles (see page 75). Alternatively, rub and press the lump of dough against a coarse grater, making pea-sized pieces.

Place the strips or pieces on foil or greaseproof paper on a baking tray and dry off in a slow oven (140°C/275°F, Gas Mark ¾) for 1½–2 hours, until dry and hard.

Store in a closed polythene bag or tin.

Serves 8–10

Savoury Tarhonya

METRIC/IMPERIAL

125 g/4 oz onions, sliced
125 g/4 oz mushrooms, sliced
2–3 tablespoons oil
125 g/4 oz tomatoes, skinned
and sliced
250 g/8 oz Tarhonya (see
previous recipe)

600 ml/1 pint boiling water
1 vegetable stock cube
1–2 teaspoons chopped herbs

Fry onions and mushrooms in oil in covered pan over low heat until light brown. Add tomatoes, Tarhonya, water and stock cube. Simmer, covered, until water is absorbed and Tarhonya is soft. Add more hot water if needed. Serve garnished with herbs.

Serves 4

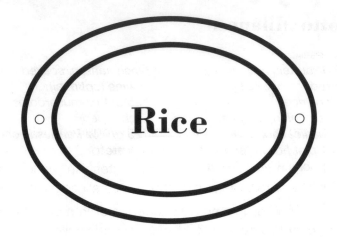

Rice

Risi e Bisi

METRIC/IMPERIAL

50 g/2 oz butter
250 g/8 oz rice
125 g/4 oz onion, chopped
600 ml/1 pint hot water
1 teaspoon salt
1 teaspoon glutamate powder
* or 1 tablespoon Tartex*

250 g/8 oz peas, fresh or
* frozen*
125–175 g/4–6 oz cheese,
* grated*
little grated nutmeg

Fry rice in oil and butter in thick pan over low heat until pale yellow. Add onion and cook 2 or 3 minutes longer. Add water, salt and glutamate powder or Tartex. Bring to boil. Add peas.

Reduce heat, cover pan and simmer gently until all liquid is absorbed and rice is just tender. Remove from heat. Stir in half the cheese. Add nutmeg and correct the seasoning. Turn into a hot serving dish. Sprinkle with a little grated cheese and hand the rest separately.

Serves 6

Risotto Milanese

Metric/Imperial

50 g/2 oz butter
2 tablespoons olive oil
250 g/8 oz rice
125 g/4 oz onion, chopped
1 clove garlic, chopped
600 ml/1 pint hot water
2 tablespoons white wine or dry sherry

pinch saffron, soaked in a little wine (optional)
125 g/4 oz mushrooms, chopped
125 g/4 oz Parmesan cheese, grated

Heat butter and oil in a heavy saucepan or iron casserole. Add rice, stir over low heat until it becomes pale yellow. This will take about 10 minutes.

Add onion and garlic. Cook 5 minutes longer. Add 300 ml/ ½ pint water, cover and cook over low heat until water is absorbed. Add saffron, wine, remaining water and mushrooms. Stir rice. Cover and continue cooking until all liquid is absorbed. Remove from heat. Stir in cheese and turn into a hot serving dish.

Serves 4

Variations:
Risotto Napolitana: Omit mushrooms, wine and saffron. Add 250 g/8 oz ripe, skinned and sliced tomatoes and 1 teaspoon fresh or dried thyme to the rice, along with the onion and garlic.
Easy Risotto: Substitute 2 level tablespoons tomato purée for tomatoes in Risotto Napolitana. Omit garlic and herbs if preferred.

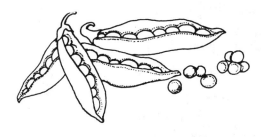

Vegetarian Pilaff

METRIC/IMPERIAL

250 g/8 oz brown rice
1 tablespoon vegetable oil
50 g/2 oz butter or nut fat
125 g/4 oz onion, chopped
3 sticks celery
600 ml/1 pint hot water
50 g/2 oz sultanas
125 g/4 oz mushrooms,
   chopped or 6 pieces dried
   fungi or mushrooms soaked
   overnight in water
1 teaspoon yeast extract,
   savoury extract or Tartex

125 g/4 oz salted cashew nuts
   or peanuts
1 teaspoon salt and sugar
   mixed
1 teaspoon nutmeg
1 teaspoon ground ginger or
   small piece fresh root
   ginger, finely chopped
little chopped parsley
1 slice lemon

Fry rice in oil and butter in thick pan over low heat until pale brown. Add onion and celery and cook 5 minutes longer. Add water, sultanas and mushrooms. Cover and simmer until liquid is absorbed and rice just tender. Add a little more water if needed.

Stir in yeast extract or other savoury flavouring and half the salted nuts. Add seasoning and spices. Serve in a casserole. Garnish the top of the pilaff with salted nuts, parsley and lemon.

Serves 4–5

Greek Pilaff

250 g/8 oz long-grain rice
2 tablespoons vegetable oil
50 g/2 oz butter or nut fat
1 large onion, sliced
2 cloves garlic, finely chopped
250 g/8 oz tomatoes, skinned
    and sliced or 300 ml/½ pint
    canned tomatoes
125 g/4 oz dried peaches and
    prunes, stoned
50 g/2 oz seedless raisins

pinch saffron soaked in
    300 ml/½ pint hot water for
    30 minutes
juice and grated rind of
    ½ lemon
1 bay leaf
peel, cut into matchsticks, and
    juice of ½ orange
black pepper to taste
1 tablespoon savoury extract
few chopped chives

Fry rice in oil and butter over low heat in thick pan until pale yellow. Add onion and garlic. Cook 2–3 minutes longer.

Add tomatoes, fruit, water with saffron, lemon rind and juice and bay leaf. Cover and simmer until water is absorbed and rice is just tender. Add a little more water if needed.

Using a chopstick or handle of wooden spoon, stir in the orange juice, half the prepared peel, pepper and savoury extract. Serve the pilaff in a casserole. Sprinkle chopped chives and orange peel on top.

Serves 4–5

VARIATIONS: Instead of peaches and prunes, use apricots and prunes, peaches and figs or pears and apple rings.

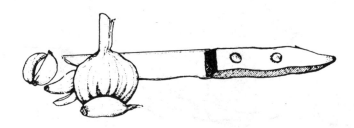

Pilaff, African-Style

METRIC/IMPERIAL

250 g/8 oz brown rice
3 medium-sized onions,
*   peeled and sliced*
4 tablespoons vegetable oil
1 level teaspoon curry powder
juice of whole and grated rind
*   of ½ lemon*
600 ml/1 pint hot water or
*   water and liquid from*
*   canned sweetcorn*
1 teaspoon salt

1 x 125 g/4 oz packet of frozen
*   sweetcorn or 1 x 300 g/10 oz*
*   can sweetcorn*
125 g/4 oz tomatoes, skinned
*   and sliced*
150 g/5 oz red pepper, seeded
*   and chopped*
125 g/4 oz salted peanuts
salt and pepper to taste
lemon slice

Fry dry rice with onion in oil in thick pan over low heat for about 5 minutes. Stir in curry powder, lemon juice and rind, hot water, salt and sweetcorn.

Cover and simmer for 20 minutes. Add tomatoes and 125 g/ 4 oz of the chopped pepper. Cook 10 minutes longer, until rice is tender and liquid absorbed. Add more water if pilaff is too thick. Stir.

Stir in half the salted peanuts. Season. Serve in the casserole or on a serving dish. Garnish with remaining red pepper and a lemon slice.

Serves 4

Turkish Pilaff

METRIC/IMPERIAL

50 g/2 oz butter or nut fat
2 tablespoons vegetable oil
250 g/8 oz rice
3 medium-sized onions, sliced
2–3 cloves garlic, chopped
pinch of saffron soaked in
    300 ml/½ pint hot water
    (optional)
1 level tablespoon finely
    chopped green root ginger
    or preserved ginger
1 heaped tablespoon grated
    fresh coconut or coarsely
    desiccated coconut

50 g/2 oz dried apricots, cut in
    strips
50 g/2 oz seedless raisins
50–125 g/2–4 oz almonds,
    blanched and split
salt and pepper to taste
300 ml/½ pint Coconut Milk
    (see page 163)
few orange slices
few spring onions or chives,
    chopped

Fry dry rice in fat and oil in thick pan or iron casserole over low heat until pale yellow. Add onions and garlic. Cook 2–3 minutes longer. Add saffron and water, ginger, coconut, apricots, raisins and almonds. Cover and simmer for 15 minutes.

Pour in Coconut Milk. Cook until rice is tender and liquid absorbed. Season. Serve in the casserole, or turned out into a hot serving dish. Garnish with orange slices and spring onions or chives.

Serves 4

VARIATIONS: Use green pistachio nuts as a garnish. For spices, use 1 teaspoon each of coriander, cardamom and fennel seeds, bruised in a pestle and mortar, tied in a little piece of muslin, cooked with the rice and removed before serving.

Instead of coconut, almonds and Coconut Milk, use cashew nuts and cashew nut milk, made by whisking 2 level tablespoons of the nut cream into 300 ml/½ pint warm water.

Spanish Rice or Vegetarian Paella

METRIC/IMPERIAL

250 g/8 oz rice
3–4 tablespoons olive oil
250 g/8 oz onions, chopped
1 large clove garlic, crushed
  with 1 teaspoon salt
250 g/8 oz tomatoes, skinned
  and chopped or 300 ml/½ pint
  canned tomatoes
pinch saffron soaked in 600 ml/
  1 pint hot water
125 g/4 oz cucumber, peeled
  and diced
3 sticks celery, chopped
125–175 g/4–6 oz red and green
  peppers, canned or fresh,
  seeded and thinly sliced

1 tablespoon chopped parsley
1 tablespoon chopped thyme
  or marjoram
1 teaspoon grated lemon rind
salt and pepper to taste
125–175 g/4–6 oz cheese,
  grated
50–125 g/2–4 oz salted nuts
few black olives, stoned or
  fried mushrooms
few thin strips red pepper

Fry dry rice in oil in thick pan over low heat until pale yellow. Add onions, garlic and salt and cook 2–3 minutes more.

Add tomatoes and water. Cover and cook over low heat for 15 minutes. Add cucumber and celery. Cook 5 minutes longer.

Stir in peppers, using a chopstick or handle of a wooden spoon. Cook about 5 minutes longer until rice is just tender and liquid absorbed. Add more hot water if needed. Remove from heat. Stir in herbs, lemon rind and nuts. Correct seasoning.

Turn into an ovenproof dish. Garnish with olives and red pepper. Serve cheese separately or sprinkle some of the cheese on top and brown under the grill.

Serves 4–5

VARIATIONS: When cooked, pile into a hot dish and garnish with fried bananas and hard-boiled eggs instead of cheese.

A simpler version. Boil and drain 250 g/8 oz rice. Cook separately, onion, garlic and peppers in oil for 5 minutes. Mix together and add 2 tablespoons tomato purée and 50 g/2 oz cheese.

Kitchri

METRIC/IMPERIAL

150 g/5 oz rice
150 g/5 oz lentils
600 ml/1 pint water

1 teaspoon salt
25 g/1 oz margarine or butter
few sliced tomatoes

Wash rice and lentils in a strainer under cold water tap. Cook slowly in covered pan with water and salt for about 30 minutes, or until water is absorbed. Stir in butter or margarine.

Serve in a hot dish, garnished with tomatoes.

Serves 3–4

Rice Fritters

METRIC/IMPERIAL

125 g/4 oz rice
300 ml/½ pint hot water
50 g/2 oz cheese, grated
1 small onion, finely chopped
 or 2 tablespoons onion soup
 mix
1 level tablespoon self-raising
 flour
2 eggs, separated

2 tablespoons milk
1 level teaspoon yeast extract
 or 2 teaspoons brewer's
 yeast powder
salt and pepper to taste
little oil for shallow frying
Tomato Sauce (see pages
 153–4) or Tomato Gravy
 (see page 156)

Simmer rice and water in covered pan for about 20 minutes. Drain, if necessary, in a strainer.

Mix together rice, cheese, onion, flour, egg yolk, milk and yeast extract to a thick batter. Season. Fold in stiffly beaten whites. Drop a tablespoonful at a time into hot oil in a frying pan and fry both sides to light brown.

Drain on kitchen paper and keep hot on a serving dish under low grill. Serve with Tomato Sauce or Tomato Gravy.

Serves 3

NOTE: Whole eggs may be mixed in but the fritters will not be so light and puffy.

Stuffed Aubergines

METRIC/IMPERIAL

2 large aubergines (about
  625 g/1¼ lb)
2 teaspoons salt
little oil for frying
1 medium-sized onion,
  chopped
1 clove garlic, chopped
175 g/6 oz rice
50 g/2 oz margarine or butter
450 ml/¾ pint hot water

2 teaspoons mixed herbs
250 g/8 oz tomatoes, sliced or
  2 level tablespoons tomato
  purée
1 egg, beaten
50 g/2 oz cheese, grated or
  25 g/1 oz cheese, grated
  and 25 g/1 oz breadcrumbs
pepper to taste

Cut aubergines in half lengthwise and run point of a knife round the edge, just inside the skin and slit in criss cross pattern. Sprinkle 1 teaspoon salt over each half. Leave 30 minutes.

Drain off liquid and fry gently, cut side down, in oil in a frying pan for about 5 minutes. Cool a little and scrape out the centre of each half, using a tablespoon. Fry onion, garlic and rice, in fat in thick saucepan over low heat for 5 minutes, stirring well. Add water, herbs, tomato and aubergine pulp. Cover and simmer until liquid is absorbed and rice just tender. Remove from heat. Stir in egg and cheese. Season.

Fill aubergine skins with the mixture. Brush skin with oil and pack stuffed halves into a greased ovenproof dish. Sprinkle tops with cheese and breadcrumbs or just cheese.

Bake on top shelf of a preheated moderately hot oven (190°C/375°F, Gas Mark 5) for 15 minutes or grill under low heat for 15 minutes.

Serves 4

Egg Dishes

Poached Eggs with Cheese Sauce

METRIC/IMPERIAL
3 eggs
Cheese Sauce (see page 158)

If using a poaching pan, have greased patty pans ready over water that is just boiling. Drop 1 egg into each pan, cover and simmer until set.

Alternatively, have ready a frying pan half-filled with just boiling water. Drop eggs into the pan, and simmer until just set. Remove each egg with a fish slice, and drain on a towel, or kitchen paper. Trim the ragged edges with a knife if necessary. Serve covered with Cheese Sauce.

Serves 3

NOTE: To get a better shape, drop the eggs into 5–7-cm/2–3-inch pastry cutters, standing in the pan of just boiling water. When cooked remove egg and cutter with fish slice. Drain, then remove cutter.

VARIATION: Serve with Mushroom Sauce (see page 157), or Curry Sauce (see page 163–5), instead of Cheese Sauce.

Vegetarian Scotch Eggs

METRIC/IMPERIAL

1 medium-sized onion, finely
  chopped
900 ml/1½ pints oil
1 level tablespoon flour
150 ml/¼ pint hot water
1 level tablespoon tomato
  purée
2 teaspoons mixed dried herbs
2 teaspoons yeast extract
125 g/4 oz milled cashew nuts
125 g/4 oz milled other nuts,
  eg walnuts, peanuts

50 g/2 oz breadcrumbs
125 g/4 oz mashed potato
little beaten egg or milk
4 hard-boiled eggs
50 g/2 oz breadcrumbs
4 grilled tomatoes
few fried mushrooms
Tomato Sauce (see pages
  153–4) or Onion Gravy (see
  page 158)

Fry onion in 2 tablespoons oil. Stir in flour and water to make a thick sauce. Add tomato purée, herbs and yeast extract. Remove from heat. Add nuts, bread, potato and egg or milk to make a firm mixture.

With oiled hands, wrap some of the mixture round each egg to a thickness of 1 cm/½ inch and shape to a cylinder. Brush with beaten egg and shake each one in a bag or bowl with breadcrumbs until well coated. Press crumbs in firmly.

Heat oil in a deep frying pan to 190°C/375°F. Place eggs one by one in hot fat using a perforated spoon with a long handle. Cook until light brown all over. Remove with spoon and drain on paper. Cut in halves with a sharp knife. Arrange standing on end on a dish.

Serve hot, garnished with tomatoes or mushrooms, greens and Tomato Sauce or Onion Gravy. Alternatively, serve cold, garnished with cress, with salad, rolls or jacket potatoes and butter.

Serves 4

Jing Dun Steamed Eggs

METRIC/IMPERIAL

2 eggs, beaten

2 teaspoons dry sherry

1 teaspoon vegetable oil

pinch salt, pepper and sugar

few chives, chopped (optional)

150 ml/¼ pint water

1 tablespoon soy sauce

Stir all other ingredients into eggs. Steam in two greased bowls or small fireproof glass dishes for about 10 minutes until firm. Serve with soy sauce on top, with thin toast.

Serves 2

Oeufs à la Crème

METRIC/IMPERIAL

4 tablespoons cream (double, single, top of milk or evaporated milk)

pinch salt, black pepper, and grated nutmeg

4 eggs

Put cream and seasonings into two buttered pots. Break 2 eggs into each pot.

Stand pots in tin of water and bake on top shelf of a preheated hot oven (200°C/400°F, Gas Mark 6) for 10 minutes, or stand covered pots in saucepan of water reaching half way up their sides. Simmer until set.

Serve hot or cold with toast and glass of tomato juice.

Serves 2

NOTE: You will need 150-ml/¼-pint size fireproof pots with lids, or special glass pots with clip-on lids which can be immersed in a pan of hot water.

Savoury Baked Eggs with Cream

METRIC/IMPERIAL
125 g/4 oz mushrooms, sliced
4 tablespoons cream (double,
   single or evaporated milk)
salt and pepper to taste

1 teaspoon onion soup mix
25 g/1 oz butter
4 eggs
25 g/1 oz grated cheese

Mix mushrooms with cream, seasonings and soup mix. Put half the mixture into two 150-ml/¼-pint size fireproof dishes. Break 2 eggs into each dish. Top with cheese.

Bake on top shelf of a preheated oven (180°C/350°F, Gas Mark 4) for about 15 minutes, until set. Serve with toast or rolls and butter, tomato juice and green salad.

Serves 2

Egg Foo Yung

METRIC/IMPERIAL
375 g/12 oz mushrooms,
   sliced
40–50 g/1½–2 oz onion, sliced
40–50 g/1½–2 oz celery, sliced
50 g/2 oz butter or margarine
50–75 g/2–3 oz canned bean
   sprouts

4 eggs, beaten
2 tablespoons corn or nut oil
few lemon twists
little watercress

Gently fry mushrooms with onion and celery in butter or margarine in covered pan for 5 minutes. Add bean sprouts and cook 5 minutes longer. Cool. Stir in eggs.

Drop spoonfuls of mixture into hot oil in frying pan. Turn fritters over as soon as firm. Garnish with lemon twists and cress. Serve with soy sauce and rice.

Serve 4

de

IAL

:ed

)pers, seeded and

ed

250 g/8 oz mushrooms, thinly
   sliced
250 g/8 oz tomatoes, skinned
   and thinly sliced

1 tablespoon olive oil
1 clove garlic crushed with
   ½ teaspoon salt and
   1 teaspoon thyme
2 eggs, beaten
little watercress or lettuce

Gently fry onion, pepper, mushrooms and tomatoes in a thick, covered saucepan until tender. Add garlic, salt and thyme. Remove from heat. Add the eggs and stir until cooked. Garnish with lettuce or watercress. Serve on fried bread.

Serves 4

VARIATIONS:

Tcheckuka: Omit mushrooms and thyme. Instead use 2 cloves garlic and 3 eggs. Fry all ingredients except eggs for 15 minutes. Transfer to a casserole and bake at 160°C/325°F, Gas Mark 3 for 1½ hours. Break eggs on top. Cover and cook for an additional 10 minutes until eggs are set.
Peperonata: Substitute red for green peppers. Omit spices and mushrooms. Eggs may be cooked on top as in Tcheckuka if liked. Serve hot or cold.

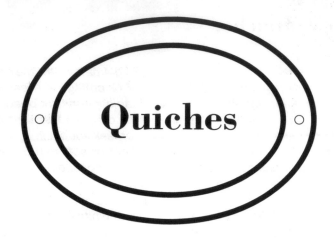

Quiches

Quiche Niçoise

METRIC/IMPERIAL

cooked pastry shell (see
   Danish Quiche, page 106)
75–125 g/3–4 oz chopped
   onion
2 tablespoons olive oil
500 g/1 lb fresh tomatoes,
   peeled and sliced or 600 ml/
   1 pint canned tomatoes
1 large clove garlic, crushed
   with 1 level teaspoon salt
1 teaspoon chopped or dried

basil, oregano or thyme
3 eggs, beaten
50 g/2 oz blue cheese,
   crumbled
pepper to taste
125 g/4 oz mixed black and
   green olives, stoned
25 g/1 oz Parmesan cheese,
   grated
1 tablespoon olive oil

Fry onion in olive oil until light brown. Add tomatoes, garlic
and herbs. Cook in covered pan for 5 minutes. Cool.

Stir in eggs and blue cheese. Mix well. Add pepper and
pour into pastry shell. Arrange olives on top, sprinkle with
Parmesan cheese and pour 1 tablespoon olive oil over. Bake
on top shelf of a preheated moderate oven (190°C/375°F, Gas
Mark 5), for about 20 minutes.

Serves 4–5

Danish Quiche

METRIC/IMPERIAL

for pastry shell:
75 g/3 oz margarine or 50 g/
   2 oz margarine and 25 g/
   1 oz nut fat
175 g/6 oz plain flour
pinch salt
2 or 3 tablespoons cold water
2 slices stale bread, diced
for filling:
50 g/2 oz Danish Blue Cheese
   (blue Cheshire, Gorgonzola
   or Roquefort may be
   substituted)

125 g/4 oz mild cheese or 200 g/
   7 oz cottage cheese
2 tablespoons chopped spring
   onion or 2 teaspoons onion
   or leek soup mix
25 g/1 oz softened butter
2 large eggs, beaten
450 ml/¾ pint milk
pinch cayenne pepper
pinch white pepper

For pastry shell:

Rub fat into flour and salt and mix to a stiff dough with water. Roll out 2.5 mm/⅛ inch thick on lightly floured board. Let stand for 5 minutes to relax.

Lift pastry, draped over the rolling pin, and lay it over a 20-cm/8-inch greased sandwich tin or flan ring. Lift edges up, and press pastry down gently, to fit into corners. Trim off surplus pastry with a sharp knife and fill with diced bread.

Bake on middle shelf of a preheated hot oven (200°C/400°F, Gas Mark 6) for 15 minutes. Remove bread. Cool a little. Place half-cooked case on baking sheet.

For filling:

Blend cheeses, soup mix and butter with a fork. Mix in eggs and finally milk and seasonings. Stir in onion and pour into pastry shell.

Bake on top shelf of a moderate oven (190°C/375°F, Gas Mark 5) for 20-25 minutes until set and brown on top.

Serves 4–5

Asparagus Quiche

METRIC/IMPERIAL

cooked pastry shell (see
    Danish Quiche, opposite)
1 x 500 g/16 oz can asparagus
1 small can evaporated milk

2 eggs, beaten
125 g/4 oz cheese, grated
salt, pepper and grated
    nutmeg to taste

Combine asparagus liquid with milk and add enough water to make up 450 ml/¾ pint. Whisk in eggs to custard texture. Season.

Cover base of pastry shell with half the cheese. Lay asparagus on the cheese. Pour liquid mixture over top. It should be three-quarters full. Top with remaining cheese.

Bake on top shelf of a preheated moderate oven (180°C/350°F, Gas Mark 4) for about 20 minutes or until it is set and feels firm in middle. Serve hot or cold.

Serves 4

Mushroom Quiche

METRIC/IMPERIAL

cooked pastry shell (see
    Danish Quiche, opposite)
375 g/12 oz mushrooms with
    stalks, sliced
25 g/1 oz butter
2 tablespoons vegetable oil
2 level teaspoons onion soup
    mix or 1 small onion, chopped
1 level teaspoon chopped

fresh ginger or ½ teaspoon
    ground ginger
2 tablespoons medium
    cooking sherry
300 ml/½ pint double cream
3 eggs, beaten
salt and pepper to taste
50 g/2 oz mild cheese
    (preferably Gruyère)

Gently cook mushrooms, fat, onion or soup mix, ginger and sherry together, in closed pan, for about 10 minutes. Cool. Stir in cream and eggs. Season.

Fill prepared pastry case. Top with grated cheese. Bake on top shelf of a preheated moderate oven (180°C/350°F, Gas Mark 4), for about 30 minutes.

Serves 4–5

Main Vegetable and Fruit Dishes

Potato Goulash

METRIC/IMPERIAL

250 g/8 oz onions, thinly sliced
2 tablespoons vegetable oil
50 g/2 oz butter or margarine
1 kg/2 lb potatoes, peeled and
   cut in 1-cm/½-inch thick slices
1 level tablespoon
   paprika
150 ml/¼ pint water
2 level teaspoons salt

1 level tablespoon flour
2 level teaspoons caraway
   seeds
150 ml/¼ pint sour cream (or
   double cream mixed with
   2 teaspoons vinegar)
few chives or spring onions,
   chopped
few hard-boiled eggs, sliced

Fry onions in oil and butter or margarine, over low heat in large saucepan (1.2–1.8-litre/2–3-pint size), until golden. Add potatoes and paprika and stir. Add water and salt. Cover and cook slowly for 20 minutes until potatoes are just soft. Stir in flour, blended with 3–4 tablespoons water, and caraway seeds. Cook a minute or two to thicken. Remove from heat.

Stir in sour cream, pile up in a casserole, sprinkle with chives or onion and egg.

Serves 4

VARIATION: Substitute 1 kg/2 lb diced marrow or pumpkin for potatoes.

Potatoes with Creamy Ch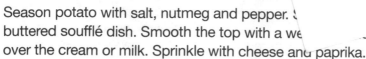

METRIC/IMPERIAL

625–750 g/1¼–1½ lb cooked
   potato, mashed or 1 packet
   instant potato
salt, pepper and nutmeg to
   taste

150 m
  150 n
  milk
175 g/6 o
1 teaspoo.

Season potato with salt, nutmeg and pepper. $
buttered soufflé dish. Smooth the top with a we   ↲ pour
over the cream or milk. Sprinkle with cheese anᴑ paprika.

Place in a tin of hot water on top shelf of a preheated hot
oven (200°C/400°F, Gas Mark 6), for 15 minutes to brown.
Finish under the grill if necessary. Serve with a salad.

Serves 4

Dahl

METRIC/IMPERIAL

1 medium-sized onion,
  chopped
250 g/8 oz lentils
3–4 tablespoons vegetable oil
1–2 tablespoons curry powder
600 ml/1 pint water

1 teaspoon yeast extract
25 g/1 oz coconut cream
1 tablespoon tomato purée or
  tomato sauce or lemon juice
few chopped chives
few hard-boiled eggs, sliced

Fry onion with lentils in oil over low low heat for 5 minutes. Stir
in curry powder, water, yeast extract, coconut cream and
tomato purée, sauce or lemon juice.

Bring to boil and simmer over low heat for about 30 minutes,
or until lentils are tender and liquid is absorbed. Stir occasionally
with chopstick or handle of wooden spoon or fork, so that lentils
are not mashed. Add more water if needed, and salt to taste.

Turn into hot serving dish. Garnish with chives and eggs.
Serve with rice.

Serves 4–5

⸍ean Pot

.AL

⸍ oz dry red beans,
⸍aked overnight in 1.2
   litres/2 pints boiled water
125 g/4 oz onions, chopped
125 g/4 oz carrots, thinly sliced
250 g/8 oz tomatoes, skinned
   and sliced or 300 ml/½ pint
   canned tomatoes
1 or 2 cloves garlic, crushed
   with 1 level teaspoon salt
2 level teaspoons paprika

3 tablespoons vegetable oil
½ teaspoon marjoram
1 x 2.5-cm/1-inch piece fresh
   chilli, finely chopped or
   ½ level teaspoon chilli powder
125 g/4 oz red pepper,
   chopped
2 teaspoons yeast extract
salt and pepper to taste
chopped parsley or spring
   onion

Put the soaked beans, and the soaking liquid into pressure cooker together with all but the last five ingredients. Cover, bring to boil and cook under pressure for 20–25 minutes.

Reduce pressure, remove lid and bring to boil. Add chilli and red pepper. Simmer, uncovered, for 10 minutes to reduce the liquid. Stir in yeast extract and season. Turn into a casserole or serving dish. Garnish with parsley or spring onion.

Serves 5–6

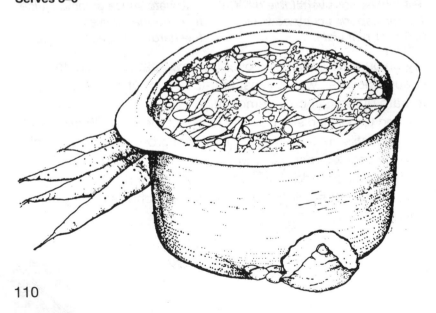

Savoury Roast

METRIC/IMPERIAL

1 x 500 g/16 oz can baked
  beans in tomato sauce
125 g/4 oz coarsely crumbled
  bread
250 g/8 oz grated cheese
2 teaspoons mixed herbs

1 onion, chopped and fried
  until transparent or
  2 teaspoons onion soup mix
1 egg or little milk if necessary
1 tablespoon oil
Rich Gravy (see page 156)

Mash baked beans in tomato sauce, with bread. Leave to stand 10 minutes.

Stir in cheese, herbs and onion. Mix well, until stiff; if not stiff enough, add a little more cheese and bread; if too stiff, add an egg or a little milk.

Pack into a well-greased 500-g/1-lb loaf tin or Yorkshire pudding tin. Brush top with oil. Bake on top shelf of a preheated oven (180°C/350°F, Gas Mark 4) for about 1 hour. It is done when it is brown, feels firm, and shrinks from side of tin.

Serve hot on a dish or cut in squares and garnished with grilled tomatoes and peas. Serve with Rich Gravy and potatoes or cold, sliced or cut in squares, garnished with radishes, cucumber and cold peas. Serve with salad and chips or new potatoes.

Serves 4

NOTE: Leftovers can be mashed with butter and used as a spread.

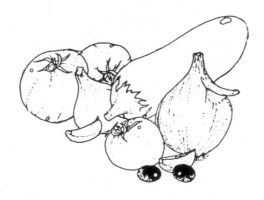

111

Mushroom Roast

METRIC/IMPERIAL

1 large or 2 medium-sized
  onions, chopped
1 green pepper, chopped
125 g/4 oz mushrooms,
  sliced
125 g/4 oz brown
  breadcrumbs

200 g/7 oz grated cheese
3 eggs
25 g/1 oz butter
seasoning to taste
pinch mixed herbs
Tomato Sauce (see pages
  153–4)

Gently fry together onion and green pepper until almost cooked. Add mushrooms and cook together for 2 minutes.

Remove from heat, add remaining ingredients except the cheese and mix thoroughly.

Grease a 20 x 10 cm/8 x 4 inch cake tin. Press the mixture into it and sprinkle with cheese and mixed herbs. Bake on middle shelf of a preheated oven (180°C/350°F, Gas Mark 4) for 45 minutes. Serve with Tomato Sauce, new or boiled potatoes.

Serves 4–5

Mushroom Pudding

METRIC/IMPERIAL

375–500 g/12 oz–1 lb
  mushrooms
2 tablespoons vegetable oil
25 g/1 oz butter
175 g/6 oz self-raising flour
3 heaped tablespoons stuffing
  mix
1 heaped tablespoon dried
  milk or soya flour

50 g/2 oz margarine or nut fat
  or 4 tablespoons oil
1 level teaspoon salt
2 level tablespoons soup mix
  (celery, onion, leek or
  mushroom) blended with
  4 tablespoons water

Gently fry chopped stalks and whole mushrooms in oil in covered saucepan for 10 minutes.

Put flour, stuffing mix, dried milk or soya flour and salt in a basin and rub in the fat or oil. Add enough water to mix to a firm dough, using a fork.

Divide the dough into two-thirds and one-third pieces. Line the 900-ml/1½-pint greased basin with the larger piece of dough, pressing it up the sides of the basin with fingers and just over the edge.

Fill lined basin with cooked mushrooms. Pour soup mix blended with water to a thin cream over mushrooms.

Flatten the smaller piece of dough to a round to fit inside top of the basin. Wet edges and bring sides over. Close by pinching the edges firmly together.

Cover with polythene or greaseproof paper. Steam 1½–2 hours, either in a steamer or standing in a saucepan of boiling water.

Serve the pudding in the basin, accompanied by greens and carrots.

Serves 4–5

Stuffed Peppers, Provençal-Style

METRIC/IMPERIAL

2 aubergines (250 g/8 oz),
  diced
1 large carrot (125 g/4 oz),
  peeled and chopped
1 large onion (125 g/4 oz),
  peeled and sliced
1 clove garlic crushed with
  1 level teaspoon salt
1 large potato (250 g/8 oz),
  peeled and diced
250 g/8 oz marrow or
  pumpkin, peeled and diced
4 tablespoons vegetable oil
4 medium-sized red or green

peppers, seeded, stalks
  removed and split
  lengthwise
1 x 300 g/10 oz can baked
  beans in tomato sauce
50 g/2 oz cheese, grated or
  2 eggs, hard-boiled
some packet stuffing or some
  breadcrumbs mixed with
  2 level teaspoons mixed
  dried herbs
little grated cheese
little chopped chives or parsley

Cook aubergines, carrot, onion, garlic, salt, potato and marrow or pumpkin in oil in a thick closed pan over low heat. Stir often to prevent sticking. Cook for about 15 minutes until vegetables are soft.

Cook peppers in boiling water for 5 minutes. Drain.

Add baked beans to vegetable mixture. Remove from heat, stir in cheese or egg and enough packet stuffing or breadcrumbs mixed with herbs to make a fairly firm, but not stodgy, mixture.

Fill peppers with mixture, press the tomato wedges into the tops and sprinkle with a little cheese. Pack into a shallow ovenproof dish.

Bake on the middle shelf of a preheated moderately hot oven (190°C/375°F, Gas Mark 5), for about 30 minutes. Serve in the dish, sprinkled with parsley or chives.

Serves 4

Stuffed Peppers or Pimentoes

METRIC/IMPERIAL

6 peppers
1 medium-sized onion,
  chopped
1 clove garlic, chopped
50 g/2 oz margarine or butter
175 g/6 oz rice
75–125 g/3–4 oz mushrooms,
  chopped
450 ml/¾ pint hot water

1 teaspoon yeast or savoury
  extract
1 level tablespoon chopped
  parsley
1 egg, beaten
salt and pepper
250 g/8 oz tomatoes, sliced
little sugar
little oil

Cook peppers in boiling water for 5 minutes. Cut off tops and scoop out seeds with a spoon.

To make the stuffing, cook onion and garlic in fat over low heat. Add rice, mushrooms, water and yeast or savoury extract. Simmer until liquid is absorbed. Mix in parsley and eggs. Cool a little. Season.

Stuff the peppers and place on an oiled, shallow ovenproof dish, surrounded by sliced tomatoes sprinkled with a little sugar, salt and pepper. Brush peppers with oil.

Bake on top shelf of a preheated moderate oven (180°C/350°F, Gas Mark 4) for about 30 minutes. Serve in the dish with French bread and butter or garlic bread.

Serves 4

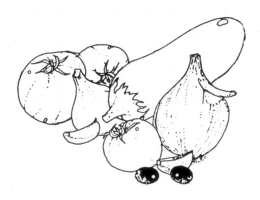

Stuffed Aubergines

METRIC/IMPERIAL

2 large aubergines (500–625 g/ 1–1¼ lb)
1 level teaspoon salt
3 tablespoons oil
1 medium-sized onion, finely chopped
125 g/4 oz brown or white breadcrumbs or 175 g/6 oz moist bread

50 g/2 oz milled or grated nuts (preferably brazil nuts)
1 rounded teaspoon mixed dried herbs
1 level teaspoon grated lemon rind
1 egg, beaten
salt and pepper to taste
50 g/2 oz cheese, grated

Cut aubergines in half lengthwise and run point of a knife round the edge, just inside the skin. Make several slits across. Sprinkle with salt and leave for 30 minutes.

Drain off liquid and fry cut side down in the oil or butter for 5–7 minutes. Scoop out the pulp with a spoon into a mixing bowl.

Fry onion in remaining oil or butter until pale yellow. Stir in the breadcrumbs, to absorb the fat.

In the mixing bowl, combine aubergine pulp, onion, bread, nuts, herbs and lemon rind. Bind with egg to a stiff mixture. Season.

Brush aubergine skins with oil and fill with stuffing. Top with grated cheese. Pack into a greased, shallow ovenproof dish. Bake on top shelf of a preheated moderate oven (180°C/350°F, Gas Mark 4) for 30 minutes. Serve with Tomato Sauce (see pages 153–4) and a green vegetable.

Serves 4

Stuffed Marrows

METRIC/IMPERIAL

1 medium-sized onion, chopped
1 clove garlic, chopped
175 g/6 oz rice
125 g/4 oz margarine or butter
125 g/4 oz mushrooms,
   chopped
450 ml/¾ pint hot water
1 teaspoon yeast extract

2 teaspoons mixed herbs
125 g/4 oz canned nut meat,
   diced or 125 g/4 oz cheese,
   grated
1 egg, beaten
1.5–2 kg/3–4 lb marrow
1 tomato, cut in 8 wedges
   chopped parsley or chives

Fry onion, garlic and rice in 50 g/2 oz fat over low heat for
5 minutes. Stir in mushrooms. Add hot water, yeast extract
and herbs. Cover and simmer until water is absorbed. The rice
need not be fully cooked. Stir in half the cheese or nut meat
and egg. Cool.

For small marrows, weighing 750 g-1 kg/1½–2 lb, split
lengthwise, scoop out seeds with spoon. Pile stuffing into
centre. Brush marrow shells with melted fat. Pack filled shells
into a shallow ovenproof dish with 2–3 tablespoons water and
cover with foil or greased paper. Bake on top shelf of a
preheated moderate oven (180°C/350°F, Gas Mark 4) for
about 40 minutes. Top should be browned.

For large marrows: Cut in 2.5-cm/1-inch thick rings, peel and
remove centres with 5–7-cm/2–3-inch pastry cutter. Cook the
rings in boiling salted water for 10 minutes. Drain. Pack the rings
in a large, shallow ovenproof dish, well greased with fat or oil.

Pile up the stuffing in the centres. Top with a tomato wedge,
pressed into the stuffing and a little grated cheese. Cover.
Bake on top shelf of a preheated moderate oven
(180°C/350°F, Gas Mark 4) for about 30 minutes. Test the
marrow with a skewer. It should be just tender.

Brown under grill if liked and serve in the dish. Sprinkle over
some chopped chives or parsley.

Serves 4–5

Marrow Neapolitan

METRIC/IMPERIAL

1 medium-sized onion, sliced
50 g/2 oz butter or margarine
3 tablespoons olive oil
250 g/8 oz tomatoes, skinned
  and sliced
1 teaspoon fresh or dry basil,
  chopped
1 teaspoon fresh or dry
  marjoram

salt and pepper to taste
little sugar
6 baby marrows or 1 kg/2 lb
  marrow
2–3 tablespoons flour
little oil
little chopped parsley
175 g–250 g/6–8 oz cheese,
  thinly sliced

Cook onion in butter and oil over low heat until transparent. Add tomatoes and herbs. Simmer in closed pan for about 20 minutes to make a thick sauce. Rub through a nylon strainer, or liquidize in a blender. Season. Add sugar.

Slice the baby marrows into rounds or cut the marrow, peeled, into 1-cm/½-inch rings and then into quarters. Shake in a bag with flour to coat then shake in a strainer to remove excess.

Fry in hot oil, turning to brown on both sides.

Put layers of marrow, cheese and tomato mixture in a shallow baking dish, finishing with tomato and cheese. Bake on top shelf of a moderately hot oven (190°C/375°F, Gas Mark 5) for about 20 minutes.

Serve in the dish, sprinkled with parsley, with French bread or rolls and butter, or green salad.

Serves 5–6

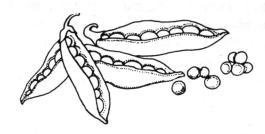

White or Mealie Pudding

METRIC/IMPERIAL

500 g/1 lb medium or pin-head
  oatmeal
250–300 g/8–12 oz onions,
  peeled and chopped
75–125 g/3–4 oz hard nut fat
  or margarine

2 level teaspoons salt
1 level teaspoon Jamaica
  pepper (allspice) or black
  pepper
Rich Gravy (see page 156)

Brown the oatmeal either on a baking sheet in a moderate oven (180°C/350°F, Gas Mark 4) or in a thick frying pan, over very low heat.

Cook onions with some of the fat in a saucepan over low heat until golden. Mix in oatmeal and seasonings.

Half fill sausage skins and tie in circles, pricking skins with a needle to prevent bursting. Or tie loosely in a pudding cloth like a dumpling. Or pack into two 1.2-litre/2-pint pudding basins, uncovered.

Boil 1–1½ hours in water to cover sausages or wrapped puddings, but reaching only half-way up sides of the basins. Serve the puddings hot with Rich Gravy and greens, or sliced and fried in a little oil until brown and crisp, with fried tomatoes and boiled swedes and carrots.

Serves 6

NOTE: Some kinds of polythene can be boiled. Tie the puddings loosely and boil in the usual way.

The liquid from the boiled puddings makes a good soup. Add sliced leeks, celery, carrots and potato to boiling liquid and simmer until soft. Add some yeast extract, thicken if needed and serve with grated cheese.

Savoury Steamed Pudding

METRIC/IMPERIAL

liquid mix:

300 ml/½ pint warm water

1 level teaspoon sugar

3 level teaspoons dried yeast
   or 25 g/1 oz fresh yeast

2 eggs

1 level teaspoon flour, white,
   wholemeal or mixed

dry mix:

375 g/12 oz plain flour, white,
   brown or mixed

50 g/2 oz fine semolina

25 g/1 oz dried skimmed milk
   or soya flour

50 g/2 oz nut fat or margarine,
   rubbed into flour

2 level teaspoons salt

3 level teaspoons mixed herbs

125 g/4 oz onion, chopped
   and lightly fried in
   1 tablespoon vegetable oil

to serve:

Rich Gravy (see page 156)

sprig parsley

500 g/1 lb peas, cooked

few grilled tomatoes

Mix water, sugar, year (if using dried yeast first mix with sugar, then add water) eggs and teaspoon flour. Tip dry mix ingredients, all at once, into mixing bowl. Mix with fork, adding more water if needed, to make a soft dough which drops off the spoon when shaken.

Half fill two large (900-ml/1½-pint size) basins, greased with nut fat or margarine.

Put the basins inside two strong polythene bags, gather up the top of the bags and tie loosely with string. Place the puddings in the steamer, standing on a piece of paper or rag to protect the polythene, fill the steamer base with cold water and stand over lowest possible heat. Turn heat off if water gets at all hot.

When puddings have risen to within 2.5 cm/1 inch of the top, turn up the heat and boil steadily for 1 hour. Serve the pudding, turned out on to a hot dish, with gravy poured round and garnished with parsley, peas and tomatoes.

Serves 10 (2 puddings)

NOTE: Two puddings can be made at the same time, one to be refrigerated for a quick meal another day. It should then be resteamed for 30 minutes.

Leftover pudding can be fried and served with gravy or diced and put into soup.

Yorkshire Season Pudding

METRIC/IMPERIAL
150 ml/¼ pint boiling milk
250 g/8 oz stale bread
1 onion, chopped
125 g/4 oz margarine or butter
1 tablespoon dried sage

salt and pepper
2 eggs
Tomato Gravy (see pages
  153–4) or Rich Gravy (see
  page 156)

Pour milk over bread in a mixing bowl.

Gently fry onion in 50 g/2 oz fat for 3 minutes. Add onion and fat from pan to mashed bread. Add seasonings and eggs. Mix well until stiff.

Melt remaining fat in a shallow Yorkshire pudding tin and put in the mixture. Press down, mark top with fork and brush with oil. Bake on middle shelf of a preheated moderate oven (180°C/350°F, Gas Mark 4) for 1–1½ hours until brown. Serve cut into squares with gravy.

Serves 4

Savoury Bread and Butter Pudding

METRIC/IMPERIAL
6 slices buttered bread
175–250 g/6–8 oz cheese,
  grated
600 ml/1 pint milk

3 eggs, beaten
salt and pepper
125 g/4 oz tomatoes, sliced

Fill a 1.2-litre/2-pint greased pie dish with layers of bread and cheese. Mix together milk, eggs and seasonings. Pour over the filled dish. Put tomatoes round the edge of the dish.

Stand the dish in a tin of water and bake on the top shelf of a preheated moderate oven (180°C/350°F, Gas Mark 4), for about 45 minutes until mixture is just set and puffy.

Serves 4 5

VARIATION: For a more savoury flavour, use 300 ml/½ pint vegetable stock instead of all milk.

Dry Potato Curry

METRIC/IMPERIAL

750 g/1½ lb potatoes, peeled
    and cut into chunks
600 ml/1 pint salted water
1 level teaspoon salt
2 tablespoons vegetable oil
25 g/1 oz butter or margarine
1 large onion, chopped
1–2 level tablespoons curry
    powder
grated rind and juice of 1 small
    lemon or 2 teaspoons
    tamarind mixed with 3
    tablespoons hot water

50 g/2 oz green pepper, finely
    chopped
1 small clove garlic crushed
    with 1 level teaspoon salt
    (optional)
125 g/4 oz salted peanuts

Parboil potatoes for 7 minutes. Drain.

Fry onion and curry powder in fat over low heat for 5
minutes. Add potatoes, half lemon rind and all the juice or
tamarind and water. Cover and cook 10–15 minutes longer.
Stir occasionally with chopstick or handle of a wooden spoon
to mix without mashing and to prevent sticking. Add garlic,
green pepper and half the nuts. Cover and cook a few
minutes longer.

Turn into a hot serving dish, sprinkle remaining nuts on top.
Garnish with cress and lemon slice. Serve with a lentil or fruit
curry, rice and a tray of relishes.

Serves 4

VARIATION: Substitute 50 g/2 oz coarsely grated coconut cream for nuts.

Potato and Tomato Curry

METRIC/IMPERIAL

1 medium-sized onion, peeled
  and chopped
4 tablespoons vegetable oil
2 level tablespoons curry
  powder
1 level tablespoon flour
500 g/1 lb tomatoes, skinned
  and sliced or 600 ml/1 pint
  canned tomatoes
1 level tablespoon fresh
  ginger, finely chopped

300 ml/½ pint hot water
1 level tablespoon sweet pickle
  or 1 tablespoon lemon juice
  and 1 teaspoon sugar
1 clove garlic crushed with 1
  level teaspoon salt
25 g/1 oz coconut cream
500 g/1 lb potatoes, boiled
  and cut into large pieces
1 hard-boiled egg, chopped
few cucumber twists

Gently fry onion in oil. Stir in curry powder and flour. Add tomatoes, ginger, water and sweet pickle or sugar and lemon juice. Simmer for 15 minutes. Mix in garlic and salt, coconut cream and potatoes.

Serve curry in a large casserole, garnished with egg and cucumber twists.

Serves 4

Curry Powder

METRIC/IMPERIAL

for flavour:
25 g/1 oz turmeric
50 g/2 oz coriander seed
25 g/1 oz cumin seed
5 g/¼ oz fenugreek
5 g/¼ oz cardamoms, husked

for strength:
5 g/¼ oz dried chillis
125 g/4 oz mustard seed
15 g/½ oz root ginger
15 g/½ oz black peppercorns

The traditional way is to pound the spices in a pestle and mortar or crush with a rolling pin on a board. The modern way is to use a coffee grinder. Grind some bread crust first to remove coffee flavour, and afterwards clean the grinder and remove curry taste. Store in a tin with an air-tight lid.

To make a mild curry use 1 teaspoonful per person and for a stronger curry flavour use 2 or 3 level teaspoons per person. If the curry flavour is too hot, stir in some cream (fresh, canned or sour) or evaporated milk just before serving.

For sweetness use a sweet chutney or pickle, sultanas, raisins, marmalade, seedless jam or sugar. For sourness, a tart apple, sour pickles, lemon, vinegar, tomato purée, tomatoes or tamarind. For a nutty taste, peanut butter, nut butters (hazel, walnut, almond, brazil), almond, cashew nut or coconut cream, ground or milled nuts.

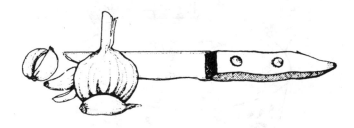

Fruit Curry Modern-Style

METRIC/IMPERIAL

900 ml/1½ pints boiling water
1 level teaspoon salt
2 heaped tablespoons
   desiccated coconut or 25 g/
   1 oz coconut cream
1 large onion (125–175 g/
   4–6 oz)
25 g/1 oz butter or margarine
2 tablespoons vegetable oil
1 level tablespoon curry
   powder
1 level tablespoon flour

½ level tablespoon ground
   ginger or 1 level tablespoon
   fresh ginger, chopped
450 ml/¾ pint fruit juice
2 teaspoons soy sauce or
   yeast or savoury extract
grated rind and juice of 1 lemon
3 x 425–500 g/14–16 oz cans
   fruit drained: pineapple,
   apricots, peaches, pears,
   mangoes, guavas (seeded)
2 tablespoons double cream

Pour water over salt and desiccated coconut. Let stand 15 minutes. Strain.

Fry onion in butter and oil, over low heat, until yellow. Stir in curry powder, flour, ginger and enough fruit juice to make a thick sauce. Add soy sauce or extract, lemon rind and juice and fruit. Simmer 5 minutes to heat through. Stir in coconut milk and cream. Add more salt if needed.

Turn into a hot dish. Serve with rice; sliced bananas mixed with frozen orange juice; salted nuts, potato crisps or poppadums; and a green salad.

Serves 4

Vegetable Curry 1

METRIC/IMPERIAL

3 tablespoons vegetable oil
175 g/6 oz carrots, peeled and
   thinly sliced
3 large sticks celery, cut in
   1-cm/½-inch lengths
1 large potato, peeled and cut
   in 2.5-cm/1-inch cubes
1 medium-sized parsnip,
   peeled and sliced

300 ml/½ pint hot water
Curry Sauce (see pages 163–5)
125 g/4 oz tomatoes, skinned
   and quartered
1 x 300 g/10 oz can baked
   beans in tomato sauce
salt and pepper to taste
50 g/2 oz salted peanuts

Heat oil in large saucepan. Add carrot, celery, potato and parsnip. Cover and cook over low heat for about 10 minutes to develop flavour. Stir frequently. Add water. Bring to boil and simmer, covered until nearly soft, this will take 7–10 minutes.

Pour in curry sauce, add tomatoes and baked beans. Cover and simmer for 10 minutes. Add more salt and pepper to taste. Turn into a hot casserole. Garnish the top with boiled rice and chutney.

Serves 4

NOTE: It is a good idea to allow 175–250 g/6–8 oz vegetables per person.

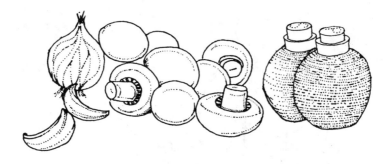

Vegetable Curry 2

METRIC/IMPERIAL

900 ml/1½ pints boiling water
25 g/1 oz coconut cream or
  50 g/2 oz desiccated
  coconut or 125 g/4 oz fresh
  grated coconut
½ teaspoon salt
250 g/8 oz aubergine, diced
250 g/8 oz cucumber, peeled
  and diced

125 g/4 oz green pepper,
  seeded and thinly sliced
250 g/8 oz cauliflower sprigs
125 g/4 oz peas, fresh or
  frozen
Curry Sauce (see pages 163–5)
pepper to taste

Pour 300 ml/½ pint water over coconut or coconut cream. Allow to stand for 30 minutes. Strain to remove coconut.

Sprinkle salt over aubergine. Spread out on a dish and leave for 15–30 minutes. Pour off liquid from aubergine and dry the dice on kitchen paper.

Add aubergine slowly to 600 ml/1 pint of boiling water but do not let the water stop boiling. Then add cucumber, pepper and cauliflower. Boil for a further 5 minutes. Add peas. Boil 5–10 minutes longer or until all the vegetables are tender.

Drain vegetables and add to curry sauce. Mix in coconut milk. Add pepper and more salt if needed.

Serve from the casserole with boiled rice in a separate dish. Hand round small dishes of chutney, sliced banana with lemon juice and salted peanuts.

Serves 4

Vegetable Casserole, Indian-Style

METRIC/IMPERIAL

3 onions, peeled and sliced
½ teaspoon turmeric
½ teaspoon cumin seeds
2 teaspoons cornflour or flour
½ green chilli, seeded, finely
  shredded
3 cloves garlic, finely chopped
175–250 g/6–8 oz green peas
  or broad beans

2 green peppers, seeded and
  cut into squares
3 large tomatoes, skinned and
  chopped
pinch salt
2 tablespoons oil
1 tablespoon lemon juice

Roll onions in turmeric, cumin and flour. Mix chilli with peas or broad beans and peppers in a bowl, and add garlic.

Place a layer of onions in a casserole. Cover with peppers and a layer of tomatoes. Sprinkle with salt and continue adding layers until all ingredients have been used up.

Pour oil over, cover with a lid and place in a preheated moderate oven (190°C/375°F, Gas Mark 5). Stew for 20–25 minutes or until cooked. Pour lemon juice over, just before serving.

Serves 4

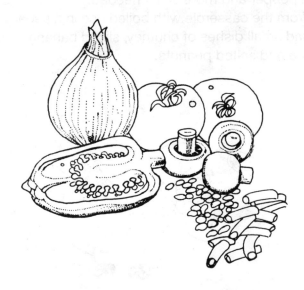

128

Vegetable Hotpot

METRIC/IMPERIAL

900 ml/1½ pints water
2 tablespoons tomato purée
50 g/2 oz lentils
125 g/4 oz dried peas or
    beans, soaked overnight in
    water
3 tablespoons vegetable oil
250 g/8 oz potatoes, peeled
    and cut into 2.5-cm/1-inch
    cubes
250 g/8 oz onions, sliced

250 g/8 oz carrots, peeled and
    sliced 5 mm/¼ inch thick
3 large sticks celery, cut in
    1-cm/½-inch pieces
125–175 g/4–6 oz cabbage,
    shredded
125 g/4 oz cauliflower sprigs
1 clove garlic, crushed with 1
    level teaspoon salt
1–2 teaspoons yeast extract
4 tablespoons evaporated milk

Collect water, tomato purée, lentils and peas or beans in a 1.2–1.8-litre/2–3-pint saucepan. Bring to the boil, then simmer until peas or beans are just soft. This will take 45 minutes–1 hour.

Fry together in oil over a low heat in 1.8–2.4-litre/3–4-pint saucepan, potatoes, onions, carrots and celery to develop flavour. Pour in the lentils, peas and their liquid. Simmer, covered, for 20 minutes.

Add cabbage and cauliflower slowly, keeping the liquid just boiling in order to preserve the green colour. Simmer 10 minutes longer. Stir in garlic, salt and yeast extract.

Remove from heat. Stir in evaporated milk. Add salt and pepper to taste. Serve in a large casserole with a bowl of chopped hard-boiled egg and chives, or a bowl of grated cheese, handed separately.

Serves 4

Creamy Vegetable Crumble

METRIC/IMPERIAL

125 g/4 oz onion, peeled and
   sliced
2 tablespoons vegetable oil
1 packet celery soup mix
150 ml/¼ pint evaporated milk
1 x 500 g/16 oz can baked
   beans

1 x 500 g/16 oz can carrots
75 g/3 oz margarine
175 g/6 oz plain flour, brown
   or white

Fry onion in oil over low heat for 5–7 minutes.

Make up half the packet of soup mix. Mix in evaporated milk.

Place beans, carrots, onion and soup in 1.2-litre/2-pint pie dish.

Make crumble by rubbing margarine into flour and the remaining dry soup mix. Sprinkle crumble on top of vegetables. Bake on middle shelf of a preheated moderate oven (180°C/350°F, Gas Mark 4) for about 40 minutes. Serve with baked tomatoes and greens.

Serves 4–5

VARIATION:
Savoury crumble: Add 50 g/2 oz grated cheese with the evaporated milk.

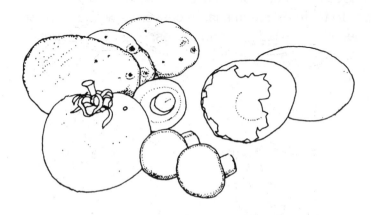

Banana Curry

METRIC/IMPERIAL

2 medium-sized onions (175 g/ 6 oz) chopped

1 medium-sized green pepper (250 g/8 oz), seeded and thinly sliced

4 tablespoons oil

2 level tablespoons curry powder

1 tablespoon peanut butter

1 tablespoon fresh ginger, chopped

2 teaspoons chilli vinegar

450 ml/¾ pint hot water

50-75 g/2–3 oz sultanas or raisins

4 large green or unripe bananas, peeled and cut into large chunks

4 eggs, hard-boiled and cut into quarters

Fry onion and pepper in oil over low heat for 3–4 minutes. Mix in curry powder, peanut butter, ginger, vinegar, water and sultanas. Stir to make a thick sauce. Add bananas. Cover and simmer for 5 minutes.

Arrange eggs on a serving dish. Pour curry on top. Serve with rice and lime chutney.

Serves 4

Maltese Curry

METRIC/IMPERIAL

500 g/1 lb onions, peeled and
   sliced thinly
3 tablespoons oil
2–3 tablespoons curry powder
500 g/1 lb tomatoes, skinned
   and sliced or 600 ml/1 pint
   canned tomatoes
300 ml/½ pint water or canned
   fruit liquid

1-2 bananas peeled and sliced
1 small can apricots, peaches
   or plums or 125 g/4 oz dried
   apricots, soaked
4 eggs, beaten
salt to taste
few lemon slices
salted nuts or walnuts

Fry onion in oil in thick pan over low heat until pale yellow. Stir in curry powder. Add tomatoes. Cover and cook for 30 minutes.

Add water or fruit liquid, bananas and apricots. Cook for 30 minutes until soft. Remove from heat and cool a little.

Stir in eggs to make a smooth mixture. Season. Pour into hot dish and garnish with lemon slices and nuts. Serve with boiled rice.

Serves 5–6

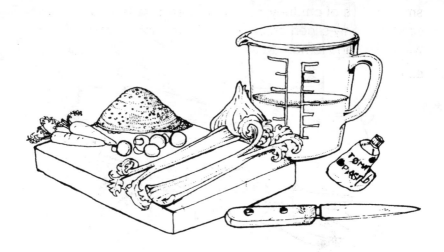

Cuban Curry

METRIC/IMPERIAL

1 medium-sized onion,
  chopped
75 g/3 oz butter or margarine
1 level tablespoon curry powder
1 level tablespoon flour
150 ml/¼ pint water
1 level teaspoon fresh or dried
  thyme
2 level tablespoons fresh or
  dried parsley

grated rind and juice of ½
  lemon
4–5 large bananas, sliced
250 g/8 oz melon, peeled and
  cut in 2.5-cm/1-inch cubes
1 level tablespoon brown
  sugar
150 ml/¼ pint nut milk (see
  pages 162 and 163)
salt to taste

Fry onion in oil and 50 g/2 oz butter or margarine over a low heat for a few minutes. Stir in curry powder, flour and water. Cook to make a thick sauce. Add herbs, loosely tied in a small piece of muslin, and lemon rind. Simmer 10–15 minutes.

Fry bananas and melon with lemon juice in the remaining butter over low heat in covered pan, stirring frequently to prevent sticking. Sprinkle in sugar. Pour in the curry sauce. Remove herbs. Stir in nut milk. Add salt.

Pour into a casserole and keep hot for 10–15 minutes so that the fruit absorbs the curry flavours. Serve with rice and small dishes of chutney, hard-boiled egg, salted nuts and a salad of thinly sliced crisp onion and roughly chopped parsley with an oil and lemon dressing.

Serves 4

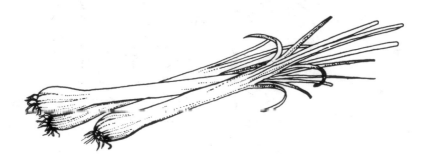

Fruitarian Curry

METRIC/IMPERIAL

375 g/12 oz dried fruit salad,
    diced
150 ml/¼ pint orange juice
450 ml/¾ pint water
50 g/2 oz sugar

300 ml/½ pint nut milk (see
    pages 162 and 163)
Curry Sauce (see page 162–5)

Soak fruit salad in orange juice and water in covered saucepan for 6 hours or more. Simmer in the pan with sugar for 15–20 minutes until fruit is soft and liquid absorbed.

To prepare nut milk: pour water over coconut or nut cream, let stand for 20–30 minutes. Drain off desiccated coconut.

Stir nut milk into Curry Sauce, then the cream and lastly the fruit. Reheat if necessary but do not boil. Add more salt and lemon juice if needed.

Pour the fruit curry into a hot serving dish. Garnish with orange twists, salted nuts and watercress. Serve with boiled rice, hot lime pickle and potato crisps or sliced water chestnuts.

Serves 4–5

Fruit Curry

METRIC/IMPERIAL

750 g/1½ lb cooking pears or apples, peeled, cored and halved

1 x 500 g/16 oz can apricots or peaches

1 small onion, chopped

3 tablespoons vegetable oil

1 tablespoon curry powder

1 level tablespoon flour

600 ml/1 pint water

1 teaspoon yeast or savoury extract

2 level teaspoons fresh ginger, chopped or 1 level teaspoon ground ginger

grated rind and juice of ½ lemon

25 g/1 oz coconut cream or ground almonds

salt to taste

2 bananas, peeled and sliced

2 tablespoons double cream

orange twists

few salted nuts or 25 g/1 oz raisins, cooked in little orange juice for a few minutes

few sprigs watercress

Simmer the pears and/or apples in the juice from the apricots or peaches in a covered pan until nearly tender.

Cook the onion in the oil over low heat until pale yellow. Stir in the curry powder, flour, water and yeast or savoury extract. Boil to thicken. Add the ginger, lemon rind and juice and nut cream or almonds. Add salt.

Mix in the cooked fruit, juice, canned fruit and the bananas. Reheat carefully to avoid sticking.

Remove from heat and stir in the cream. Add more salt if needed. Serve on a bed of rice on a large serving dish. Garnish with orange twists and watercress. Scatter a few salted nuts on the top of the curry.

Serves 4

Parsnip and Banana Curry

METRIC/IMPERIAL

500 g/1 lb parsnips, peeled
  and sliced
50–75 g/2–3 oz sultanas or
  raisins
450 ml/¾ pint water
1 medium-sized onion, peeled
  and sliced
1 green pepper, seeded and
  chopped
2 level tablespoons curry
  powder

1 level tablespoon chopped
  fresh ginger or ½ level
  tablespoon ground ginger
1 level tablespoon sugar
4 tablespoons oil
grated rind and juice of ½ lemon
1 heaped tablespoon peanut
  butter or ground almonds
1 level teaspoon salt
1 or 2 large bananas, cut in
  chunks

Cook parsnips with sultanas in the water for 10 minutes.

Cook onion and pepper in oil over low heat in a covered pan until soft. Add curry powder, ginger and sugar and cook, stirring, for a further 2 minutes.

Add strained vegetable water, lemon rind and juice and peanut butter or almonds to make a thick sauce. Add salt if necessary. Mix in parsnip, sultanas and bananas. Heat through then turn into a hot dish.

Serve with rice and little dishes of diced fresh pineapple, thinly sliced orange, mixed with chopped onion and lemon juice; and salted nuts or potato crisps as accompaniments.

Serves 4

West Indian Fruit Curry

METRIC/IMPERIAL

1 tablespoon turmeric
1 teaspoon cumin seed
1 cardamom seed, husk
   removed
1 clove
½ piece of fresh ginger,
   scraped and chopped
1 bay leaf
25 g/1 oz butter or nut fat
2 tablespoons oil
125 g/4 oz tomatoes, skinned
   and sliced

1 medium-sized onion,
   chopped finely
250 g/8 oz cooking apple,
   cored and cut in wedges
2 large bananas, peeled and
   sliced
50 g/2 oz sultanas
grated rind and juice of 1 lemon
50 g/2 oz cashew nuts or
   walnuts
1 level teaspoon salt

Cook all the spices and bay leaf in butter and oil over low heat
for 5 minutes. Stir in tomato and onion. Cover and cook for 5
minutes more. Add apple and the remaining ingredients.
Cover and cook for 10–15 minutes, until fruit is just soft.

Turn into a hot dish. Serve with rice and potato crisps or
poppadums.

Serves 3-4

137

Potato Croquettes with Mushroom Sauce

METRIC/IMPERIAL

750 g/1½ lb potatoes, boiled,
  peeled and mashed or 1
  packet instant potato, made
  up as directed
25 g/1 oz butter or margarine
4 tablespoons evaporated milk
  or 150 ml/¼ pint milk
salt, pepper and grated
  nutmeg to taste

1 egg, beaten
little hot water if needed
breadcrumbs or rolled oats for
  coating
oil for frying
Mushroom Sauce (see page
  157)
few chopped chives, spring
  onions or little cress

Mash potatoes in the saucepan with fat, milk, seasonings and egg. Beat well with a wooden spoon, adding water as needed to make a smooth mixture that is stiff enough to handle. Cool.

Divide into eight portions. Roll in the breadcrumbs or oatmeal and mould each portion to a flat oblong shape, 1 cm/½ inch thick.

Fry in hot oil until light brown on both sides. Drain. Serve with sauce poured round. Garnish with chives, onions or cress.

Serves 4

VARIATION:

Cheese and Potato Croquettes: Add 125 g/4 oz grated cheese and 1 teaspoon yeast extract to the mashed potato. Serve with Tomato Gravy (see page 157).

African Croquettes: Add to the mashed potato, 2 heaped tablespoons crunchy peanut butter or 125 g/4 oz chopped salted peanuts, 2 teaspoons yeast powder or onion soup powder and 1 teaspoon dried or fresh mixed herbs. Use 4 tablespoons evaporated milk. Garnish with grilled tomatoes or rings of red and green pepper and parsley sprigs and lemon twists. Serve with Onion Gravy (see page 157).

Nut Croquettes

METRIC/IMPERIAL

750 g/1½ lb boiled potatoes,
    mashed or 1 packet instant
    potato, made up as directed
25 g/1 oz butter
125 g/4 oz broken walnuts
1 level teaspoon curry powder
1 egg, beaten

1 heaped tablespoon dried milk
salt and pepper to taste
50 g/2 oz desiccated coconut,
    rolled oats or wheatgerm
little vegetable oil
few lemon slices
few sprigs of cress

Combine potatoes in the pan with butter, walnuts, curry powder, egg and milk. Beat well with wooden spoon to make a smooth mixture, adding some fresh milk as needed. The mixture should be stiff enough to handle. Cool.

Divide into eight portions, and roll each in chosen coating. Shape in 1-cm/½-inch thick flat oblongs. Gently fry in hot oil, browning both sides. Drain.

Serve croquettes piled on a hot dish, garnished with lemon slices and sprigs of cress.

Serves 4

German-Style Potatoes

METRIC/IMPERIAL

1 kg/2 lb new or small
    potatoes, boiled and peeled
375 g/12 oz cottage cheese
300 ml/½ pint sour cream (or
    double cream and yogurt,
    mixed)

250 g/8 oz onions, finely
    chopped
1 tablespoon chives
2-3 tablespoons caraway
    seeds

Serve potatoes hot in a bowl with the cheese. The sour cream, onions and chives and caraway seeds should be served in four smaller bowls as accompaniments.

Serves 4

Pommes Dauphinoise

METRIC/IMPERIAL
500 g/1 lb peeled potatoes,
   thinly sliced
2–3 cloves garlic, finely
   chopped or crushed with a
   little salt

1 teaspoon sea salt
1 teaspoon black pepper
300 ml/½ pint double cream

Put potatoes into boiling, salted water and cook for 2 minutes.
Drain. Pack the potato slices into a shallow ovenproof dish in
layers with salt and garlic and freshly ground pepper. Pour the
cream over the mixture.

Bake on top shelf of a preheated hot oven (200°C/400°F,
Gas Mark 6) for about 30 minutes until brown or finish by
browning under the grill. Baste the top of the potatoes with a
little cream if they become too dry.

Serves 4

Carelian-Style Potatoes

METRIC/IMPERIAL
750 g/1½ lb new or small
   potatoes
2–3 hard-boiled eggs
125 g/4 oz butter or margarine

1 level tablespoon chives or
   caraway seeds
salt and pepper to taste

Boil potatoes. Drain and put into a hot casserole.

Press eggs through a wire strainer. Cream butter or
margarine. Work in egg. Add chives or caraway seeds and
season. Pile up in a pottery or wooden bowl and serve with
the potatoes and a green salad.

Serves 4

Potato Pancakes

METRIC/IMPERIAL

3–4 tablespoons flour, plain or self-raising

2 level teaspoons salt

1 egg

2 tablespoons evaporated or powdered milk

500 g/1 lb potatoes, peeled and grated coarsely

1 small onion, finely chopped (optional)

1 teaspoon dried mixed herbs (optional)

oil for frying

few parsley sprigs and tomato wedges

Add flour, salt, egg and milk to potato to make a thick batter. Add more flour, fresh milk or water, if needed. Mix in onion and herbs, if liked.

Drop tablespoonfuls of the potato batter, one at a time, into hot oil in a large frying pan. Flatten each pancake with back of spoon, to about 7-10 cm/3–4 inches in diameter. Turn and brown both sides. Drain. Stack on a dish and keep hot.

Serve garnished with parsley or cress and tomatoes.

Serves 4

Beans in Tomato Sauce

METRIC/IMPERIAL

125–250 g/4–8 oz onions,
  chopped
50 g/2 oz fat
250 g/8 oz tomatoes, peeled
2 tablespoons black treacle
300 ml/½ pint water
6 cloves
2 bay leaves

1 level teaspoon salt
500 g/1 lb haricot beans (dry
  weight), soaked 6–12 hours
  in 1.2 litres/2 pints water
1 rounded tablespoon flour
1 rounded tablespoon dried
  skimmed milk powder
little cold water

Method 1

Put onions, fat, tomatoes, treacle, water, cloves, bay leaves, salt, soaked beans and the soaking liquid, into a pressure cooker. Cover and bring to boil. Cook under pressure for 20 minutes. Cool to bring down pressure.

Remove lid and stir in flour and milk powder, blended to a cream with a little cold water. Boil to thicken. Add more salt if needed.

Method 2

Steam beans until soft. This will take about 45 minutes.

Gently fry onions in oil for 3 or 4 minutes, do not brown. Add tomatoes, water, treacle, cloves, bay leaves and salt. Simmer for 30 minutes. Add beans. Simmer 5 minutes longer. Stir in blended flour and milk powder, into beans and sauce. Boil to thicken. Season to taste.

Serves 8

NOTE: Baked Beans in Tomato Sauce will keep one week in refrigerator or several months in deep freeze.

Creamed Beans

250 g/8 oz haricot or butter beans, soaked overnight in cold water

125 g/4 oz dried peas, as above

125 g/4 oz onions, sliced

125 g/4 oz carrots, peeled and diced

125 g/4 oz red or green peppers, seeded and thinly sliced

4 tablespoons vegetable oil

600 ml/1 pint water

1 level teaspoon salt

½ level teaspoon ground ginger or nutmeg

2 level tablespoons flour blended with little cold water

150 ml/¼ pint evaporated milk

pepper to taste

soy sauce to taste

parsley or chopped chives or grilled halved tomatoes or hard-boiled eggs, chopped

Steam beans and peas until soft for about 45 minutes or cook for 20 minutes in pressure cooker.

Cook prepared vegetables in oil, over low heat in covered pan for 15 minutes, stirring to prevent sticking. Add water, salt and ginger. Simmer 5 minutes longer. Stir in flour, blended to a cream with a little cold water. Boil to thicken. Stir in milk. Add beans and peas while hot. Season with more salt if needed, pepper and soy sauce. Turn into a serving dish or casserole. Garnish with parsley, chives, tomatoes or eggs.

Serves 4–5

VARIATION: Alter the flavour by using herbs, such as thyme and marjoram or mixed herbs, instead of the ginger.

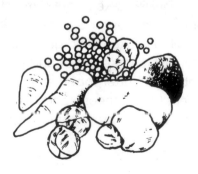

Curried Beans

METRIC/IMPERIAL

250 g/8 oz haricot beans (dry
   weight)
600 ml/1 pint Curry Sauce
   (sees page 163–5)

125 g/4 oz sultanas
salt to taste
squeeze lemon juice

Soak beans in cold water overnight. Steam for about 45 minutes until soft, or cook in the liquid in pressure cooker for 20 minutes. Use a blender or rub sauce through a strainer.

Simmer beans and sultanas in the Curry Sauce over low heat for 15–30 minutes. Add salt and lemon juice to taste.

Serves 4

NOTE: Curried Beans will keep in refrigerator 3–4 days or in deep freeze 1-2 months.

French-Style Aubergines

METRIC/IMPERIAL

3 aubergines (625–750 g/1¼–
   1½ lb), sliced 5 mm/¼ inch
   thick
salt
1 tablespoon flour blended with
   2–3 tablespoons cold water
2–3 tablespoons oil

500 g/1 lb tomatoes, skinned
   and sliced
1–2 cloves garlic crushed with
   1 level teaspoon salt
50 g/2 oz breadcrumbs
25 g/1 oz butter or margarine
25 g/1 oz cheese, grated

Salt aubergines lightly. Coat with flour. Fry in oil, turning to brown both sides. This will take about 5 minutes. Add tomatoes. Cover and simmer for 5 minutes. Stir in blended flour and water. Boil to thicken. Add garlic and salt. Place in a shallow ovenproof dish and keep hot under low grill.

Stir breadcrumbs and butter together in a pan over low heat until fat is absorbed. Mix in cheese and spread over the vegetable mixture. Grill until brown and crisp.

Serves 4

Artichoke Pastry

METRIC/IMPERIAL

1 level teaspoon salt
½ level teaspoon black pepper
½ level teaspoon grated
  nutmeg
1 kg/2 lb Jerusalem artichokes,
  peeled and cut into
  5-mm/¼-inch slices
600 ml/1 pint boiling, salted
  water

50 g/2 oz butter or margarine
2 tablespoons vegetable oil
2 slices brown bread, roughly
  crumbed
50 g/2 oz cheese, grated
pinch paprika or chopped
  parsley

Mix seasonings together.

Cook artichokes in boiling salted water until just soft. Drain. Add the butter or margarine and seasoning mixture. Place in a shallow ovenproof dish.

Mix oil and breadcrumbs together in a hot pan until crumbs have absorbed the fat. Add grated cheese. Sprinkle on top of the artichokes. Bake on top shelf of a preheated moderate oven (180°C/350°F, Gas Mark 4), for about 30 minutes until the top is brown and crisp or grill under low heat for about 20–30 minutes. Serve in the dish, with a sprinkle of paprika or parsley on top.

Serves 4–5

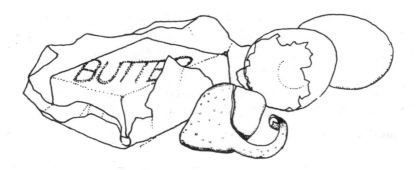

Alsacian Red Cabbage

METRIC/IMPERIAL

2 tablespoons oil
1 medium-sized onion, sliced
2 tablespoons vinegar
1 level tablespoon sugar
750 g/1½ lb red cabbage,
   shredded
600 ml/1 pint boiling water
125 g/4 oz prunes, stoned

125 g/4 oz cooking apples,
   diced
2 level teaspoons cornflour
a little cold water or red wine
   (optional)
1 level teaspoon salt
pinch mixed spices

Heat oil in thick pan over low heat. Fry onion until transparent.
Add vinegar, sugar, cabbage, water, prunes and apple.
Simmer in covered pan, stirring often. When the cabbage is
just tender, cook without a lid, to reduce water.

Add cornflour blended with cold water or wine. Boil to
thicken. Add mixed spices, salt and more sugar and more
vinegar to taste.

Serves 4

Russian-Style Asparagus

METRIC/IMPERIAL

1 x 500 g/16 oz can asparagus,
   drained
1 small can evaporated milk
2 eggs, beaten

75–125 g/3–4 oz grated cheese
salt and pepper to taste
little grated nutmeg
25 g/1 oz butter

Combine asparagus liquid and milk. Make up to 450 ml/¾ pint
with water. Mix with eggs. Season. Pour mixture over asparagus
in a buttered fireproof dish and top with grated cheese.

Bake on top shelf in a preheated moderate oven
(180°C/350°F, Gas Mark 4), for about 30 minutes until set.
Serve with brown bread, toast and green salad.

Serves 4

Cauliflower with Tomato Sauce

METRIC/IMPERIAL

750 g/1½ lb cauliflower,
  trimmed
50–75 g/2–3 oz cheese, grated

Tomato Sauce (1), omitting
garlic and wine or sherry
(see page 153)

Remove outer leaves of cauliflower, cut the stalk short and make a deep cross in it. Or, for quicker cooking, cut into large sprigs and chop inner leaves in 2.5-cm/1-inch lengths. Soak in salted water for 10 minutes.

Put cauliflower into boiling water with stalk downwards, if to be cooked whole. Cook for about 15 minutes until tender when pierced with a skewer. Drain in a colander and place on a hot dish.

Stir grated cheese into the hot sauce, and pour over the cauliflower.

Serves 4

VARIATION:

Celeriac with Tomato Sauce: Instead of cauliflower use 1 kg/2 lb boiled celeriac cut like chips and mixed with 50 g/2 oz butter and 1 tablespoon savoury extract.

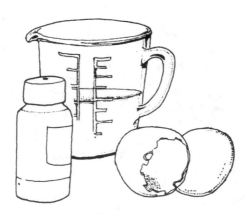

Tuscan-Style Mushrooms

METRIC/IMPERIAL

*750 g/1½ lb tomatoes, sliced
or 1 x 625 g/20 oz can
tomatoes*
*2 tablespoons vegetable oil or
25 g/1 oz butter*
1 level teaspoon salt
2 level teaspoons sugar
1 bay leaf

*500 g/1 lb mushrooms, peeled
and sliced*
2 tablespoons olive oil
*2–3 cloves garlic, crushed with
little salt*
*1 teaspoon fresh marjoram,
chopped or dried*

Cook the tomatoes with vegetable oil or butter, salt, sugar and bay leaf in a closed pan for 1 hour. Remove bay leaf. Liquidize or rub through a nylon sieve.

Simmer the mushrooms in the sauce, with olive oil, garlic, salt and marjoram for about 30 minutes until the mushrooms are tender.

Serve with plain, boiled pasta, and grated cheese; or with a vegetable platter of cooked green vegetable, carrots, new potatoes and peas. Hand grated cheese separately.

Serves 4–5

Creamed Sprouts and Chestnuts

METRIC/IMPERIAL

500 g/1 lb fresh chestnuts or
 250 g/8 oz dried chestnuts
 soaked in cold water
 overnight
500–750 g/1–1½ lb medium-
 sized sprouts
50 g/2 oz margarine or butter

1 tablespoon oil
50 g/2 oz flour
600 ml/1 pint hot milk
2 level teaspoons salt
½ level teaspoon white pepper
½ level teaspoon nutmeg, grated
little paprika

Steam chestnuts for 30 minutes or boil in 1.2 litres/2 pints of water until soft. Keep hot in pan. Alternatively make a slit in skins of fresh chestnuts and bake in a tin on top shelf of a hot oven (200°C/400°F, Gas Mark 6) for 20 minutes. Remove shells and inner skin. Steam or boil for a further 10 minutes until just soft. Keep hot in covered pan.

Remove any yellow outer leaves and slit stems of sprouts. Drop them one by one into fast-boiling water, to keep their colour. Cook for 10 minutes. Drain.

Meanwhile, prepare the sauce by cooking butter, oil and flour together until foamy. Stir in milk and beat well to make a smooth sauce. Bring just to the boil to thicken. Stir in the seasonings. Add a little water, if sauce is too thick.

Place chestnuts and sprouts in a hot serving dish. Pour the sauce on top. Garnish with paprika.

Serves 4–5

VARIATION:

Vegetable Platter: Serve sprouts and chestnuts with stuffed mushrooms and grilled tomatoes.

Scalloped Onions

METRIC/IMPERIAL

6 large onions, peeled and
   sliced
50 g/2 oz butter
3 tablespoons vegetable oil
1 level tablespoon yeast
   powder or 1 teaspoon yeast
   extract

½ level teaspoon black pepper
1 level teaspoon salt
50–75 g/2–3 oz breadcrumbs
50 g/2 oz cheese, grated
pinch paprika
little chopped parsley

Cook onion in 25 g/1 oz butter and all of the oil over a low
heat in covered pan until pale yellow. Stir in yeast powder or
extract and seasonings. Place in a shallow baking dish.

Melt remaining butter in the pan and stir in the crumbs to
absorb the fat. Remove from heat and stir in the cheese.

Spread cheese and crumb mixture on top of the onions.
Bake on top shelf of a preheated moderately hot oven
(190°C/375°F, Gas Mark 5) for about 30 minutes until brown
and crisp or cook under low grill. Sprinkle with paprika and
parsley.

Serves 4–5

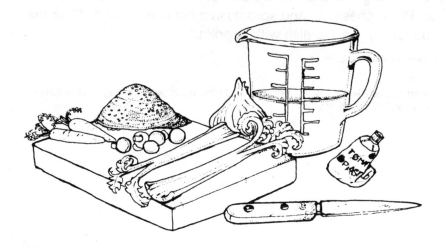

Scalloped Mixed Vegetables

METRIC/IMPERIAL

½ stick celery (including tops),
  chopped

2 tablespoons corn oil

50 g/2 oz mushrooms, washed
  and thinly sliced

1 x 300 g/10 oz can
  sweetcorn, drained

1 level teaspoon salt

½ level teaspoon black pepper

½ level teaspoon ground
  ginger

2 level teaspoons cornflour
  blended with 150 ml/¼ pint
  milk

25 g/1 oz butter

50–75 g/2–3 oz fresh
  breadcrumbs

50 g/2 oz cheese, grated

Cook celery in oil in closed pan over low heat for about 15 minutes. Stir occasionally with a wooden spoon.

Mix together the salt, pepper and ginger. Add mushrooms, sweetcorn and seasoning mixture. Stir in cornflour and milk. Boil to thicken. Pour into greased, shallow ovenproof dish.

Melt butter and stir in the breadcrumbs until fat is absorbed. Remove from heat. Mix in cheese. Sprinkle over the vegetable mixture. Bake on top shelf of a preheated moderate oven (180°C/350°F, Gas Mark 4) for about 30 minutes until the top is brown and crisp or grill under low heat for same length of time.

Serves 3–4

Chinese Stir-Fry Vegetables

METRIC/IMPERIAL

2 tablespoons oil
1 small onion, chopped
2 outer sticks celery, chopped
1 medium-sized carrot, cut in
    thin slices

250 g/8 oz cabbage, shredded
½ level teaspoon salt
pinch ground ginger or
    chopped fresh ginger

Heat oil in thick pan. Fry onion, celery and carrot, covered, over high heat, for 1 minute. Add cabbage and seasonings. Cover and fry, shaking occasionally, for 4 minutes. Serve at once.

Serves 4

NOTE: Other vegetables can be cooked this way, for example, peppers, swedes and sprouts.

Ratatouille

METRIC/IMPERIAL

4 tablespoons oil
1 large Spanish onion
2 green peppers, seeded and
    sliced
2 aubergines, sliced
500 g/1 lb courgettes, sliced or
    500 g/1 lb marrow, diced

6 tomatoes or 1 x 425 g/
    14 oz can tomatoes
1 teaspoon sugar
1 teaspoon salt
pinch marjoram or oregano
1 clove garlic (optional)
chopped parsley

Heat oil in thick pan and fry onion and pepper over low heat for 5 minutes. Add aubergine and fry 5 minutes longer. Add the rest of the vegetables, sugar, salt, marjoram or oregano and garlic. Simmer in closed pan until vegetables are soft but not mushy. Serve hot or cold, sprinkled with parsley.

Serves 4

VARIATION: If no marrows are available, frozen or canned sliced French beans can be used.

Sauces and Toppings

Tomato Sauce 1

METRIC/IMPERIAL

2 tablespoons oil
1 medium-sized onion,
   chopped
1 medium-sized carrot, grated
1 stick celery
500 g/1 lb tomatoes, sliced
1 clove garlic, crushed with
   1 level teaspoon salt
600 ml/1 pint water

1 bay leaf
1 teaspoon mixed herbs
1 teaspoon sugar
25 g/1 oz cornflour or
   arrowroot blended with little
   cold water
salt and pepper to taste
75 ml/⅛ pint Marsala wine or
   sweet cooking sherry if liked

Heat oil in a saucepan and fry vegetables over low heat with garlic and salt. Add water, herbs and sugar. Simmer for 20 minutes in covered pan. Rub through nylon strainer into a bowl. Return to pan and stir in blended cornflour, or arrowroot. Boil to thicken. Season. Stir in wine or sherry.

Serves 6

NOTE: This sauce can be stored in thick polythene bags in deep freeze.

VARIATIONS: Instead of mixed herbs use one of the following combinations: basil and marjoram or oregano; parsley, thyme, pinch grated lemon rind and mint.

Tomato Sauce 2

METRIC/IMPERIAL

2 tablespoons vegetable oil
2 level tablespoons cornflour
   or arrowroot
300 ml/½ pint tomato juice
300 ml/½ pint water
1 tablespoon tomato purée
1 level tablespoon onion soup
   powder

1 teaspoon sugar
1 level teaspoon mixed herbs
1 bay leaf
salt and pepper to taste
little savoury extract or soy
   sauce to taste

Stir oil and cornflour or arrowroot together over low heat for
1–2 minutes. Stir in tomato juice, water, purée, soup powder
and sugar. Bring to the boil, whisking well. Simmer for 5
minutes. Add seasonings and savoury extract. Pour through a
nylon strainer to remove herbs.

Serves 6

Tomato Sauce 3

METRIC/IMPERIAL

1 x 150 g/5 oz can
   concentrated tomato purée
600 ml/1 pint water
2 teaspoons sugar

1 teaspoon salt
1 bay leaf
2 tablespoons oil or 25 g/1 oz
   butter

Simmer all ingredients together for about 15 minutes.

Serves 4–6

Red-brown Tomato Sauce

METRIC/IMPERIAL

600 ml/1 pint canned
   tomatoes or 500 g/1 lb
   drained fresh tomatoes,
   skinned and sliced
125 g/4 oz onion, chopped
125 g/4 oz apple, peeled,
   cored and sliced

300 ml/½ pint brown vinegar
1 level teaspoon ground ginger
   or chopped fresh ginger
1 level teaspoon ground cloves
75–125 g/3–4 oz sugar

Cook tomatoes, onions and apple until soft. Liquidize or rub through a nylon strainer with wooden spoon.

Cook tomato pulp with vinegar, spices and sugar, stirring well, until thick. Bottle while hot.

Serves 4–6

VARIATION:

For a clear red sauce: use white vinegar, grated rind and juice of 1 lemon and ½ level teaspoon cayenne pepper or 1 teaspoon ginger. Omit cloves.

Creamy Tomato Sauce

METRIC/IMPERIAL

600 ml/1 pint Tomato Sauce
   (see pages 153–4)
4 tablespoons evaporated milk
   or 3 tablespoons double
   cream

Cool the sauce a little. Whisk in milk or cream. Keep hot in double saucepan over low heat or sauce will curdle.

Serves 6

Tomato Gravy

METRIC/IMPERIAL

125 g/4 oz tomatoes or
  150 ml/¼ pint canned
  tomatoes, sliced
25 g/1 oz butter
1 level teaspoon cornflour
  blended with 1 tablespoon
  cold water

pinch mixed herbs
1 teaspoon sugar
salt and pepper to taste

Fry tomatoes in butter for 5 minutes. Stir in blended cornflour and boil to thicken. Add herbs, sugar, salt and pepper.

Serves 4

Rich Gravy

METRIC/IMPERIAL

1 medium-sized onion,
  chopped
1 tablespoon vegetable oil
300 ml/½ pint water
1 tablespoon tomato purée

1 tablespoon smooth peanut
  butter
1 teaspoon yeast extract
salt and pepper to taste

Fry onion gently with oil in a saucepan. Add water, tomato purée and yeast extract. Bring to boil. Stir in peanut butter to thicken. Season.

Serves 4

Mushroom Sauce 1

METRIC/IMPERIAL

125 g/4 oz onions, thinly sliced
2 tablespoons vegetable oil
250 g/8 oz mushrooms, sliced
300 ml/½ pint water or milk
  and water
2 teaspoons cornflour,
  blended with 2 tablespoons
  cold water

1 level teaspoon ground
  ginger, or fresh ginger, finely
  chopped
1 teaspoon yeast extract or
  1 tablespoon soy sauce
salt and pepper to taste
2 tablespoons cooking sherry
  (optional)

Gently fry onions in oil in a thick saucepan for 5 minutes. Add mushrooms and simmer, covered, for 10 minutes longer. Add water and bring to the boil. Stir in cornflour and ginger. Boil to thicken. Stir in yeast extract or soy sauce. Add salt, pepper and sherry.

Serves 4

Mushroom Sauce 2

METRIC/IMPERIAL

125 g/4 oz mushrooms, sliced
25 g/1 oz butter
2 teaspoons flour or cornflour
4 tablespoons evaporated milk

1 can condensed mushroom
  soup
dash sherry (optional)

Gently fry mushrooms in butter for 5 minutes. Blend flour or cornflour, evaporated milk, condensed soup and sherry in a pan. Boil to thicken.

Serves 4

NOTE: This recipe also works with celery or other condensed vegetable soups.

Onion Gravy

METRIC/IMPERIAL

250 g/8 oz onions, chopped
   finely
3 tablespoons oil
1 teaspoon sugar
1 teaspoon salt

1 tablespoon cornflour or flour
   blended with 300 ml/½ pint
   cold water
1 teaspoon yeast extract
salt and pepper to taste

Gently fry onions in oil with sugar and salt until brown. Stir in blended cornflour or flour. Boil to thicken. Stir in yeast extract. Season. For a smooth gravy, rub through a strainer.

Serves 4

VARIATION: Substitute 1 tablespoon peanut butter for cornflour or flour.

Cheese Sauce

METRIC/IMPERIAL

150 ml/¼ pint evaporated milk
1 teaspoon cornflour blended
   with 1 tablespoon water
125 g/4 oz Cheddar or
   Cheshire cheese, grated

pinch nutmeg
salt and pepper to taste
1 teaspoon savoury extract or
   soy sauce

Mix evaporated milk with blended cornflour and water in a saucepan. Boil to thicken. Remove from heat and cool a little. Stir in cheese, nutmeg, salt, pepper and savoury extract or soy sauce.

Serves 3

Cheese Batter

METRIC/IMPERIAL

75 g/3 oz plain flour
1 level teaspoon salt
2 eggs
450 ml/¾ pint milk
125 g/4 oz onion, chopped

2 tablespoons oil
250 g/8 oz cheese, cut into
cubes
3–4 sage leaves, chopped or 1
teaspoon dried sage

Mix flour, salt and eggs to a smooth paste with wooden spoon. Stir in enough milk to make a thick cream, a little thicker than for pancakes.

Fry onion in oil until golden. Pour contents of frying pan into 1.5-litre/2½-pint greased pie dish. Pour in batter and drop in cheese. Sprinkle with sage. Bake on top shelf of a preheated moderately hot oven (200°C/400°F, Gas Mark 6), for 30–40 minutes.

Serve with fried or baked tomatoes, a rich gravy, green vegetables and potatoes.

Serves 4

White Sauce

METRIC/IMPERIAL
25 g/1 oz plain flour
300 ml/½ pint milk
25 g/1 oz butter or margarine
  or 2 tablespoons oil
salt and pepper to taste

Method 1

Blend flour with a little cold milk to a cream in 600-ml/1-pint bowl.

Boil remaining milk with fat. Pour onto blended flour. Stir. Return sauce to pan, stir, bring to boil and season.

Method 2

Cream flour and fat together with wooden spoon in warmed bowl. Stir in hot milk, beating or whisking to remove any lumps. Return sauce to pan, stir, bring to boil and season.

Method 3

Cook flour and fat together in thick pan over low heat until foamy. Stir in hot milk. Beat or whisk to remove lumps. Bring to boil, stirring or whisking well. Season.

Serves 4

NOTES: 125 g/4 oz butter rubbed lightly into 150 g/5 oz plain flour and 1 teaspoon salt until it looks like crumbs will keep stored in jar or tin with lid, in dark cool place.

To make white sauce, sprinkle 2 rounded tablespoons of the mixture into 300 ml/½ pint warm milk. Stir to mix. Bring to boil, stirring well. Season.

Walnut Sauce

METRIC/IMPERIAL
50 g/2 oz shelled walnuts
2 tablespoons chopped parsley
1 teaspoon sea salt
25 g/1 oz margarine or butter
2 heaped tablespoons fresh
    breadcrumbs

2 tablespoons olive oil
1–2 tablespoons double cream
1 teaspoon lemon juice
seasoning to taste

Pour boiling water over walnuts and remove as much brown skin as possible. Pound nuts, parsley and salt to a paste in a pestle and mortar, adding fat gradually. Work in crumbs and oil slowly to make a smooth paste. Finally, work in cream and lemon juice. Season. Serve as a dip, spread or sauce.

Serves 4

Savoury Nut Sauce

METRIC/IMPERIAL
125 g/4 oz onion, peeled and
    chopped
50 g/2 oz margarine or 4
    tablespoons vegetable oil
1 teaspoon sugar
2 rounded tablespoons
peanut butter
450 ml/¾ pint water

1 clove garlic, crushed with
    1 level teaspoon salt
2 teaspoons curry powder
grated rind and juice of
    ½ lemon
1–2 teaspoons yeast extract or
    soy sauce
salt and pepper to taste

Gently fry onions and sugar in fat until brown. Add peanut butter, water, garlic, curry powder, yeast and lemon. Stir over low heat to make a thick sauce. Add water from cooking vegetables to make a pouring sauce. Serve with vegetables.

Serves 4

Pistou Sauce

METRIC/IMPERIAL

4–6 cloves garlic
125 g/4 oz cheese, grated
4 tablespoons tomato purée

1 tablespoon dried basil or
  4 tablespoons fresh,
  chopped basil
150 ml/¼ pint good olive oil

Pound together garlic and cheese in a pestle and mortar. Then add tomato purée and basil, until a smooth paste. Beat in oil gradually.

Serves 4

VARIATION: Crush garlic with pinch salt in a bowl with a wooden spoon. Work in the cheese and oil.

Nut Cream

METRIC/IMPERIAL

1 heaped tablespoon nut
  cream (50 g/2 oz)

150 ml/¼ pint warm water
1 teaspoon honey

Shake nut cream, water and honey in a screw-topped jar or liquidize in a blender. This will make a thick cream. Thin down with cold water if required.

Serves 4

Coconut Cream

METRIC/IMPERIAL

300 ml/½ pint hot water
175 g/6 oz coconut, finely
  grated

Soak coconut in water for 30 minutes. Press through a strainer and skim off the creamy layer.

Serves 5

Coconut Milk

METRIC/IMPERIAL
300 ml/½ pint hot water
50 g/2 oz desiccated coconut
  or 125 g/4 oz fresh coconut,
  grated

Pour water over coconut in a bowl. Let stand for 30 minutes. Then strain through a piece of muslin draped over a strainer. Squeeze out every drop. This milky liquid has a specially delicate flavour and should be added to curry just before serving.

Serves 4

NOTE: For quicker results, whisk or liquidize 25 g/1 oz coconut cream and 300 ml/½ pint hot water together.

Curry Sauce 1

METRIC/IMPERIAL
1 medium-sized onion,
  chopped
3 tablespoons vegetable oil
1–2 tablespoons curry powder
1 tablespoon flour
600 ml/1 pint water

1 level teaspoon yeast extract
1 teaspoon sugar
juice and grated rind of ½ lemon
2 level tablespoons peanut
  butter
salt to taste

Fry onion in oil, over low heat until yellow. Add curry powder and flour. Cook 1 or 2 minutes to develop flavour. Add water, yeast extract, sugar, lemon and peanut butter. Stir to blend and thicken. Add salt. For a smooth sauce, liquidize or rub through a strainer or sieve.

Serves 4

NOTE: This sauce will keep in a polythene bag or container in the deep freeze.

VARIATIONS: To vary the flavour, use tomato purée or tomato sauce instead of lemon; sweet chutney instead of sugar. For a thin curry sauce, omit the flour.

Curry Sauce 2

METRIC/IMPERIAL

2 medium-sized onions,
  peeled and chopped
3 tablespoons vegetable oil
125 g/4 oz sour cooking
  apples, sliced
1–2 tablespoons curry powder
1 ripe banana
300 ml/½ pint water

grated rind and juice ½ lemon
1 level tablespoon marmalade
2 teaspoons cornflour blended
  with 2 tablespoons cold
  water
1 clove garlic crushed with
  1 teaspoon salt

Gently cook onion with oil, apple, curry powder and banana, in covered pan for 5–7 minutes. Stir in water, lemon and marmalade. Simmer for 10 minutes. Liquidize or rub through a strainer.

Reheat and thicken the sauce with cornflour, blended with 2 tablespoons cold water. Add garlic and salt.

Serves 4

Curry Sauce 3

METRIC/IMPERIAL

1 medium-sized onion, finely
  chopped
4 tablespoons vegetable oil
2 tablespoons curry powder
2 teaspoons cornflour
300 ml/½ pint water
1 tablespoon finely chopped
  fresh ginger

grated rind and juice of
  ½ lemon
1 tablespoon marmalade,
  seedless jam or sugar
salt to taste
2 tablespoons cream (double
  or sour)

Gently fry onion in oil until yellow. Add curry powder and cornflour. Cook 1 minute longer. Stir in water. Boil to make a thick sauce.

Mix in ginger, lemon rind and juice, marmalade, jam or sugar and salt. Cover and simmer for 10 minutes. Stir in cream.

Serves 4

Curry Sauce 4

*1 small onion or shallot, finely
 chopped*
25 g/1 oz butter or margarine
*1 level tablespoon curry
 powder*
1 level tablespoon flour
150 ml/¼ pint tomato juice
300 ml/½ pint water
*1 rounded tablespoon ground
 almonds*

1–2 teaspoons lemon juice
2 level teaspoons sugar
salt and pepper to taste
*2–3 tablespoons cream
 (double or sour)*
few cucumber twists
few lemon twists

Fry onion in butter until yellow. Add curry powder and flour. Stir in tomato juice and water mixed with ground almonds. Bring to boil. Add lemon juice and sugar.

Liquidize or rub through a strainer with a wooden spoon to make a smooth sauce. Reheat. Season. Remove from heat and stir in cream.

Serves 4

Plum Sauce

METRIC/IMPERIAL

500 g/1 lb stoneless plum jam
300 ml/½ pint vinegar
1 level teaspoon salt

1 level teaspoon ground cloves
1 level teaspoon ginger
1 level teaspoon cinnamon

Cook all ingredients together for about 10 minutes. Bottle whilst hot. The mixture thickens on cooling.

Makes 500 g/1 lb

NOTE: Store in wide-mouthed bottles, well washed, rinsed in hot water and drained. When cold, seal tops of filled bottles with hot melted candle wax, using a teaspoon.

Toffee Topping

METRIC/IMPERIAL

50 g/2 oz butter or margarine *75–125 g/3–4 oz bread, diced*
2 heaped tablespoons syrup

Melt butter and syrup. Stir in the bread.

Serves 4

NOTE: Use with fruit: spread over fruit and cook under low grill until brown
and crisp.

Coconut Crisp

METRIC/IMPERIAL

50 g/2 oz butter or margarine *2 heaped tablespoons coarsely*
25 g/1 oz soft brown sugar *desiccated coconut*
1 level tablespoon syrup
2 heaped tablespoons
cornflakes

Melt butter, sugar and syrup. Stir in cereal and coconut.

Serves 5

NOTE: Use with fruit: spread over fruit and brown under low grill.

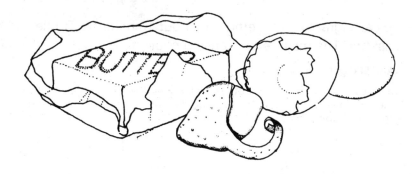

Chocolate Spread

METRIC/IMPERIAL

75 g/3 oz Basic Spread Mix (see page 25)
2–3 rounded tablespoons cocoa
1 rounded tablespoon condensed milk or milk powder

1 rounded teaspoon black treacle
1–2 tablespoons boiling water
vanilla or rum flavouring or grated orange rind to taste

Beat ingredients well together until light coloured and creamy, adding more boiling water if needed. Serve on fruit bread, buns, biscuits or sponge cake.

Serves 3

Caramel Milk Spread

METRIC/IMPERIAL

1 large can condensed milk
50 g/2 oz unsalted butter

1 rounded tablespoon frozen concentrated orange juice

Boil unopened can of milk for 2 hours. Cool, then open the tin. Beat all ingredients together to a smooth caramel cream.

This spread goes especially well with fruit bread and in a Victoria sandwich.

Serves 6

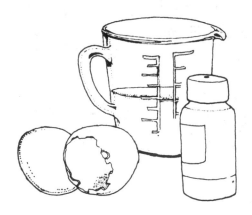

Pickles and Relishes

Spiced Vinegar 1 (mild)

METRIC/IMPERIAL

1.8 litres/3 pints vinegar
5 g/¼ oz cloves
5 g/¼ oz allspice

5 g/¼ oz cinnamon stick
5 g/¼ oz ginger root
5 g/¼ oz white peppercorns

Method 1

Tie whole spices in muslin bag. Bring vinegar and spices to the boil. Simmer in tightly covered pan for 30 minutes. Cool and bottle.

Method 2

Pressure cook loose whole spices with 600 ml/1 pint of vinegar for 15 minutes. Cool. Strain with nylon strainer and mix with 1.2 litres/2 pints vinegar.

Makes 1.8 litres/3 pints

Spiced Vinegar 2 (aromatic)

METRIC/IMPERIAL

1.8 litres/3 pints vinegar
5 g/¼ oz coriander seeds
5 g/¼ oz allspice
5 g/¼ oz cardamom seeds

5 g/¼ oz cinnamon stick
5 g/¼ oz cloves
6 bay leaves

Method as for Spiced Vinegar 1, opposite.

Makes 1.8 litres/3 pints

Spiced Vinegar 3 (hot, mixed)

METRIC/IMPERIAL

1.8 litres/3 pints vinegar
15 g/½ oz mustard seed
5 g/¼ oz allspice
5 g/¼ oz cloves

5 g/¼ oz black peppercorns
1 or 2 dried chillis or 40 g/
  1½ oz mixed pickling spice

Method as for Spiced Vinegar 1, opposite.

Makes 1.8 litres/3 pints

Red Cabbage

METRIC/IMPERIAL

1.5 kg/3 lb red cabbage
75 g/3 oz block salt or 50 g/2 oz
sea salt

1.8 litres/3 pints Spiced
Vinegar (see pages 168–9)

Remove coarse outer leaves of cabbage. Cut out stalks. Roll up big leaves and cut into 5-mm/¼-inch shreds. Cut off top of cabbage, press cut side down on board and slice as for cabbage salad, but in thicker shreds.

Put layers of cabbage and salt in deep bowls, allowing approximately 25 g/1 oz salt per 500 g/1 lb cabbage. Let stand overnight.

Drain cabbage in a colander. Pack into 500 g/1 lb jars but not too tightly. Cover with cold, spiced vinegar. Tie down tightly with thick polythene or waxed paper. Store in a cool, dark place.

Makes six 500 g/1 lb jars

NOTE: This pickle is ready to eat in a week and will keep 4–6 months.

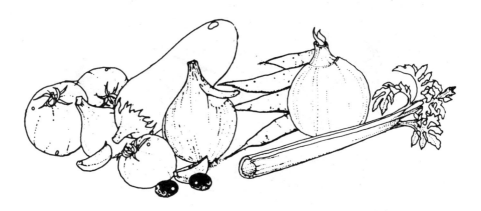

Pickled Cucumbers

METRIC/IMPERIAL

600 ml/1 pint vinegar
300 ml/½ pint water
1 teaspoon salt
1 teaspoon calcium chloride
125 g/4 oz white sugar

1.5 kg/3 lb cucumber, sliced,
* or if small whole*
1½ tablespoons mixed pickle
* spices*

Place cucumber in deep bowl. Combine vinegar, water, salt, calcium chloride, sugar and pour over cucumbers to cover. Place a plate or lid on top and leave overnight.

Collect drained liquid in large saucepan. Add spices. Bring to the boil. Add cucumbers and simmer for 10 minutes. Cool. Pack into jars and seal or cover with waxed paper.

Makes four 500 g/1 lb jars

NOTE: Store calcium chloride in a screw-top jar. If lid is not airtight it will absorb moisture from the air and become liquid. It can still be used in this form.

VARIATIONS: Substitute 500 g/1 lb sliced onion for cucumber and use 2 tablespoons mustard seed and 1 tablespoon celery seeds instead of mixed pickle spices.

Substitute for mixed pickle spices, 2 bay leaves, 1 level tablespoon mustard seed and 1–2 cloves garlic.

Pickled Prunes

METRIC/IMPERIAL

750 g/1½ lb prunes
900 ml/1½ pints brown vinegar
12 cloves
1 x 1-cm/½-inch piece root
   ginger, dried and crushed or
   1 x 1-cm/½-inch piece fresh
   ginger, scraped and
   chopped

300 ml/½ pint vinegar
250 g/8 oz brown sugar

Soak prunes overnight in brown vinegar, cloves and ginger. Cook gently until soft in closed pan.

Boil 300 ml/½ pint vinegar and sugar for a few minutes. Add to prunes and cook 5 minutes longer. Cool. Pack prunes into jars with spices. Pour in liquid and cover.

Makes 1–1.5 kg/2–3 lb

NOTE: These are a useful garnish for pizzas, salads, open sandwiches and curry. They are especially good with cheese and cottage cheese.

Mixed Vegetable Pickle

METRIC/IMPERIAL

600 ml/1 pint spiced vinegar (see pages 168–9)
cauliflowers: small sprigs, cut into1-cm/½-inch chunks and peeled stalk into slices
cucumbers: 1-cm/½-inch thick slices, halved or quartered
marrow: 1-cm/½-inch thick slices, peeled, seeded and cut in chunks

green tomatoes: whole, small, pricked with fork; or large ones, skinned and quartered
carrot: 2.5-mm/⅛-inch thick slices, peeled
onions: whole, small, peeled and cut in thick slices
celery: outer stalks, peeled and cut into 2.5-cm/1-inch pieces
300 ml/½ pint plain vinegar

Weigh prepared vegetables. Allow 1 tablespoon salt per 500 g/1 lb. Put layers of mixed vegetables and salt in deep bowls. Leave overnight.

Add 300 ml/½ pint plain vinegar to drained vegetables to remove excess salt. Drain again. Use this vinegar to wash another batch. Pack into jars and cover with spiced vinegar.

Makes 1 kg/2 lb

VARIATION: To make sweetened pickles, add artificial sweetener to vinegar, to taste.

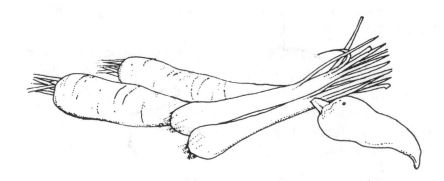

Pickled Peaches

METRIC/IMPERIAL

600 ml/1 pint white vinegar
375 g/12 oz white sugar
5-cm/2-inch cinnamon stick
8 cloves, crushed

300 ml/½ pint water
1.5 kg/3 lb small peaches,
  skinned and stoned

Simmer vinegar, sugar, spices and water for 10 minutes. Add enough peaches to be covered by liquid. Simmer until tender. Pack cooked peaches into jars. Cook rest of peaches in liquid in same way. Fill all jars with liquid and seal.

Makes 2 kg/4 lb

VARIATIONS: Use 2 x 625 g/20 oz cans peaches instead of fresh peaches and peach juice instead of water.
    Alternatively, use dried peaches: soak 750 g/1½ lb dried peaches and spices in vinegar and water in closed saucepan overnight. Simmer gently until fruit is tender. Add 500 g/1 lb brown sugar and cook gently for about 10 minutes. Proceed as above.

Piccalilli

METRIC/IMPERIAL

3 kg/6 lb mixed prepared
  vegetables (see ingredients
  for Mixed Vegetable Pickle,
  page 173)
50 g/2 oz flour
50 g/2 oz dry mustard

25 g/1 oz turmeric
1 teaspoon ground ginger
125–175 g/4–6 oz sugar or
  sweetener tablets to taste
2.4 litres/4 pints hot vinegar

Mix dry ingredients to a thin cream with 6 tablespoons vinegar in a mixing bowl. Stir in remaining vinegar. Stir and boil until thick, in a deep aluminium or stainless steel saucepan.

    Simmer vegetables in the sauce for 15 minutes, stirring occasionally. Pack into jars and cover when cold with thick polythene or waxed paper.

Makes 3.5 kg/7 lb

NOTE: Leftover Piccalilli can be mixed into a curry, white sauce, mayonnaise or salad cream and served with cooked beans and other vegetables.

Green Tomato Chutney

METRIC/IMPERIAL

500 g/1 lb apples, peeled,
  cored and sliced
500 g/1 lb sultanas
2 kg/4 lb green tomatoes,
  sliced
500 g/1 lb onion, sliced
1 level tablespoon salt
900 ml–1.2 litres/1½–2 pints
  vinegar

1 level tablespoon ground
  ginger or fresh ginger,
  chopped
1 level tablespoon curry
  powder
500 g/1 lb sugar

Cook fruit, onions and salt with 300 ml/½ pint vinegar in
closed pan over low heat until soft. Add spices, mixed with
sugar and 600 ml/1 pint vinegar. Simmer and stir until thick.
Add another 150 ml/¼ pint vinegar if needed.

Makes 3–3.5 kg/6–7 lb

NOTE: If the seal is not air-tight, the chutney darkens at the top of the jar. To
prevent this, pour a teaspoon of hot candle wax over the top, tipping the jar
to seal the surface all over. Cover with polythene.

Fresh Uncooked Chutney

METRIC/IMPERIAL

75 g/3 oz onion, chopped
  finely
juice and grated rind of
  1 lemon
50 g/2 oz currants, washed

125 g/4 oz sugar
175 g/6 oz cooking apples,
  unpeeled, cored and diced
  small
little white vinegar

Mix all ingredients together and moisten with vinegar.

Makes 500 g/1 lb

NOTE: This chutney is especially good with curries and with cheese.

VARIATION: Mix in 1 tablespoon of finely chopped fresh root ginger or
preserved ginger, and add pinch ground cardamom seeds.

Banana and Parsnip Chutney

500 g/1 lb parsnips, peeled,
  sliced and quartered if large
1.5 kg/3 lb firm bananas, not
  too ripe, sliced thinly
900 ml–1.2 litres/1½–2 pints
  white vinegar
500 g/1 lb white sugar

8 oz currants or sultanas,
  washed and picked
1 rounded tablespoon curry
  powder
1 level tablespoon ground
  cinnamon
3 level teaspoons salt

Steam or boil parsnips until just soft. Cook all ingredients in closed pan for 15 minutes, then slowly in open pan, stirring often to evaporate water, until thick. Bottle while hot.

Makes 2–2.5 kg/4–5 lb

NOTE: This chutney can be made with bananas only. It will keep about 4 weeks.

Date Chutney

1 kg/2 lb dates, stoned
250 g/8 oz onions, chopped
250 g/8 oz sultanas
250 g/8 oz sugar
600–900 ml/1–1½ pints brown
  vinegar

2 level teaspoons salt
6 red chillis
2 teaspoons fresh ginger,
  chopped or ground

Soak dates in vinegar overnight. Cook all ingredients together in closed pan over low heat for about 30 minutes, stirring frequently to make a soft, thick mixture.

Makes 1–1.5 kg/2–3 lb

VARIATION: To make a mild date chutney, use 1 level teaspoon each of ground cloves, cinnamon, ginger and cardamom and omit chillis.

Lemon Chutney

METRIC/IMPERIAL

500 g/1 lb lemons
250 g/8 oz onions, chopped
250 g/8 oz currants
500 g/1 lb white sugar

900 ml/1½ pints white vinegar
2 level teaspoons salt
12 peppercorns
12 chillis

Squeeze juice from halved lemons. Mince shells or chop finely. Cook all ingredients together in closed pan over low heat for about 30 minutes or in pressure cooker for 10 minutes, until soft and thick. Remove spices and pack into jars. Cover with hot wax, then with polythene.

Makes 1.5 kg/3 lb

VARIATION: For Mild Lemon Chutney, use 1 x 1-cm/½-inch piece fresh or dried root ginger and 6 cardamom seeds with husks removed and omit peppercorns and chillis.

Chutney-in-a-Hurry

METRIC/IMPERIAL

250 g/8 oz raisins
500 g/1 lb onions, chopped
juice and rind of 1 lemon,
    minced or chopped
600 ml/1 pint vinegar
1 level tablespoon salt

2 kg/4 lb jam, mixed or plain
2 level teaspoons ground
    cloves
2 level teaspoons cinnamon
2 level teaspoons ginger
2 level teaspoons allspice

Cook raisins, onions and rind in vinegar until soft. Add salt, jam and spices. Stir and simmer. The consistency should not be too thick.

Makes 3 kg/6 lb

Coconut, Carrot and Orange Relish

METRIC/IMPERIAL

2 rounded tablespoons
    desiccated coconut
125–150 g/4–5 oz carrot,
    grated

juice and little grated rind of
    1 small orange

Mix all ingredients together and garnish with an orange slice.

Serves 4

Lemon Relish

METRIC/IMPERIAL

75 g/3 oz tart apples, cored
    and diced
25 g/1 oz currants, washed
25 g/1 oz onion, finely
    chopped

25 g/1 oz granulated sugar
grated rind and juice of
    1 lemon

Mix all ingredients together.

Serves 4

Cucumber Relish

METRIC/IMPERIAL

1 x 10-cm/4-inch piece
    cucumber, peeled and diced
1 small onion, finely chopped
50 g/2 oz green pepper,
    seeded and finely chopped

150 ml/¼ pint yogurt
1 tablespoon double cream
salt and pepper to taste
1 teaspoon lemon juice

Mix all ingredients together.

Serves 4

Salads and Salad Dressings

Continental Cabbage Salad

METRIC/IMPERIAL

*250 g/8 oz cabbage, prepared
    as for Cabbage and Lemon
    Salad, page 181*
*125 g/4 oz small tomatoes,
    skinned*
50 g/2 oz black olives, stoned

1–2 tablespoons olive oil
1 tablespoon lemon juice
½ level teaspoon sugar
cress
*little fresh thyme or marjoram,
    chopped*

Collect all ingredients in a polythene bag and shake together.
Tip into a salad bowl. Garnish with cress. Add thyme or
marjoram.

Serves 4

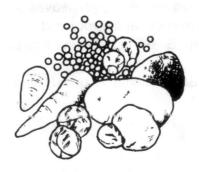

Cardinal Salad

METRIC/IMPERIAL

175 g/6 oz red cabbage, finely
  shredded
2 tablespoons vinegar
1–2 tablespoons oil
2 level teaspoons sugar

50 g/2 oz seedless raisins
125 g/4 oz cooked beetroot,
  diced
peel and diced flesh of
  1 orange

Collect all ingredients, except orange, in a polythene bag. Shake to mix.

Cut orange rind into matchsticks. Add orange to salad. Shake to mix. Turn into salad bowl, sprinkle orange peel onto the top.

Serves 4

Crunchy Salad

METRIC/IMPERIAL

250 g/8 oz cabbage, prepared
  as for Cabbage and Lemon
  Salad, opposite
25 g/1 oz green pepper,
  seeded and thinly sliced
1 small onion, finely chopped

2 sticks celery, chopped
2 tablespoons salad cream
1 tablespoon vinegar
1 or 2 packets potato crisps
few radishes

Collect in a polythene bag, cabbage, pepper, onion, celery, salad cream and vinegar. Shake to mix. Add potato crisps and shake once more.

To make radish roses, trim green leaves down to 1 cm/ ½ inch. Make a cross cut at the root end of each radish, about 1 cm/½ inch down. Soak in cold water and they will open out like roses.

Turn Crunchy Salad into salad bowl. Garnish with radishes and serve at once.

Serves 4

Cabbage and Lemon Salad

METRIC/IMPERIAL
250 g/8 oz cabbage
grated rind and juice of 1 small
    lemon
1 level teaspoon sugar

50 g/2 oz salted peanuts
lemon twist
few sprigs of cress

Cut off the top of the cabbage. Press it firmly, cut side down, on chopping board. Shred finely using a saw-edged, stainless steel knife. Soak cabbage in ice cold water for 30 minutes. Drain in colander. Dry on a tea-towel or muslin.

Store in a polythene bag, closed with a rubber ring, or in plastic container with lid, in any cool place. To serve, add lemon and sugar and shake or mix well. Tip into a salad bowl. Sprinkle nuts on top. Garnish with lemon twist and watercress.

Serves 4

VARIATION:
Nutty Salad: Substitute pinch of curry powder, 25 g/1 oz raisins and 25 g/ 1 oz broken walnuts instead of peanuts.

Caraway Cabbage Salad

METRIC/IMPERIAL
2 level teaspoons caraway
    seeds
2 tablespoons oil
1 tablespoon vinegar
1 level teaspoon French
    mustard
1 level teaspoon sugar

pinch salt and pepper
250 g/8 oz cabbage prepared
    as for cabbage and lemon
    salad, above
little pickled red cabbage, if
    liked

In a screw-top jar collect caraway seeds, oil, vinegar, mustard, sugar and seasonings. Shake well to mix. Pour over cabbage in a salad bowl and mix. Garnish with a spoonful of pickled red cabbage on top.

Serves 4

Children's Salad

METRIC/IMPERIAL

250 g/8 oz cabbage, prepared
  as for Cabbage and Lemon
  Salad, page 181
1 medium-sized carrot
  (75–125 g/3–4 oz)
50 g/2 oz mild cheese, diced
  or coarsely grated

1 eating apple, peeled and
  diced
50 g/2 oz seedless raisins
1 level teaspoon sugar
grated rind and juice of 1 lemon
little cress

Using potato peeler, cut few ribbons from carrot for garnish. Grate the rest on coarse grater.

Collect all ingredients except cress in a polythene bag and shake to mix. Turn into a salad bowl. Top with cress and garnish with carrot ribbons. Arrange potato crisps round edges of the bowl.

Serves 4

Coleslaw

METRIC/IMPERIAL

1 carton yogurt
2-3 tablespoons double cream
1 rounded teaspoon sugar
2 tablespoons vinegar

pinch salt
250 g/8 oz cabbage, prepared
  as for Cabbage and Lemon
  Salad, page 181

Mix together in salad bowl, yogurt, cream, sugar, vinegar and salt. Add cabbage and stir well to mix. Chill.

Serves 4

Coconut, Carrot and Raisin Salad

METRIC/IMPERIAL

50 g/2 oz raisins
150 ml/¼ pint canned orange
  juice

1 large carrot (250 g/8 oz),
  grated
50 g/2 oz coconut

Gently cook raisins in orange juice for 5 minutes to swell
them. Cool. Mix together carrot, coconut, raisins and orange
juice. Chill. Serve with a creamy mayonnaise.

Serves 4

Lettuce Salad

METRIC/IMPERIAL

150–175 g/5–6 oz lettuce, cos
  or iceberg broken into
  pieces
2 tablespoons parsley, roughly
  chopped
1 tablespoon chopped chives

1 level teaspoon French
  mustard
pinch salt, sugar and pepper
2 tablespoons oil
1 tablespoon lemon juice or
  vinegar

Pile lettuce in the bowl. Sprinkle parsley and chives on top.
   Shake together, in screw-top jar, mustard, seasonings, oil
and lemon juice or vinegar. Pour over salad. Toss until each
leaf is coated with dressing and serve.

Serves 4

VARIATIONS:
Continental: Add a small clove or piece of garlic and crush with pinch salt
in the salad bowl using a wooden spoon.
English Style: Add grated rind of ½ lemon to the salad dressing. Mix
1 teaspoon finely chopped thyme with parsley and chives.

Sauerkraut Salad

METRIC/IMPERIAL

1 small onion, finely chopped
175 g/6 oz sauerkraut
1 teaspoon caraway seeds

1-2 tablespoons olive oil
few chopped chives
pinch paprika

Mix all ingredients together in a basin. Pile up in a salad bowl
and garnish with paprika and chives. This salad is especially
good with cheese.

Serves 4

NOTE: Sauerkraut, a useful source of vitamin C, can be served hot, as a
vegetable, or cold as a salad. It will keep for a week in the refrigerator in a
closed container.

Fennel and Lemon Salad

METRIC/IMPERIAL

1 large root fennel, cut into
   thin matchsticks
1 lemon (125 g/4 oz), seeded
1 tablespoon parsley, finely
   chopped
1 tablespoon lemon juice

2 tablespoons olive oil
2 tablespoons double cream
2 level teaspoons sugar
freshly ground black pepper
   and salt to taste

Soak fennel in ice-cold water to crisp. Drain and dry on a
kitchen towel or paper.

Cut rind of lemon into thin strips. Peel off pith from rest of
lemon and slice flesh into thin slices. Then cut into quarters.

In salad bowl combine lemon juice, oil, cream, sugar and
seasoning to taste. Add fennel, parsley, lemon flesh and peel.
Toss in remaining ingredients.

Serves 4

Bean Salad

METRIC/IMPERIAL

125 g/4 oz red beans (dry
  weight)
125 g/4 oz haricot beans (dry
  weight)
1 level teaspoon French
  mustard
1 level teaspoon salt

2 tablespoons oil
1 tablespoon vinegar
1 small onion, chopped
1 tablespoon chopped parsley
1 or 2 hard-boiled eggs,
  chopped

Soak beans in boiled water overnight. Steam until soft for
about 45 minutes, or pressure cook in soaking liquid for
15 minutes. Drain and keep hot.

In salad bowl, mix together mustard, salt, oil and vinegar.
Add beans and mix well. When cool, stir in onion, parsley and
hard-boiled eggs.

Serves 4

Walnut and Lemon Lettuce Salad

METRIC/IMPERIAL

25 g/1 oz broken walnuts,
  crushed lightly
½ level teaspoon curry powder
pinch sugar
2 tablespoons oil

grated rind and juice of
  ½ lemon
150–175 g/5–6 oz lettuce,
  broken into pieces

Collect walnuts, curry powder, sugar, oil and lemon rind and
juice in salad bowl. Mix in nuts. Pile lettuce on top. Toss to
mix.

Serves 4

Orange, Tomato and Chicory Salad

METRIC/IMPERIAL

125 g/4 oz orange, peeled and
  seeded
500 g/1 lb chicory, cut into
  thick rings or broken into
  leaves
125 g/4 oz tomatoes, skinned
  and diced
2 tablespoons olive oil

1 tablespoon lemon juice or
  white vinegar
1 small clove garlic (optional),
  crushed with 1 level
  teaspoon salt
½ level teaspoon sugar
25 g/1 oz cress

Cut orange rind into matchsticks. Slice orange thinly.

Collect chicory, tomato and orange in salad bowl.

Collect in a screw-top jar, oil, vinegar, garlic, salt and sugar. Shake to mix. Pour dressing over salad and mix. Sprinkle with orange peel shreds. Garnish edges with cress.

Serves 5

NOTE: Chicory is crisp and appetizing, but is low in Vitamin C.

VARIATION: Add some stoned black olives.

Rice Salad

175 g/6 oz dry long-grain rice
  or 375 g/12 oz boiled rice
1 small onion, finely chopped
3 sticks celery, finely chopped
  or 50 g/2 oz celeriac, finely
  chopped
50–125 g/2–4 oz tomatoes,
  skinned, seeded and
  chopped
25 g/1 oz pickled cucumber,
  gherkins, chopped

2–3 tablespoons mayonnaise
  or salad cream
1 tablespoon cream, double,
  single or from top of milk
1 teaspoon vinegar or lemon
  juice
salt and pepper to taste
few chopped chives
chopped parsley or cress

Simmer rice over low heat with water to cover until just tender. Drain and cool.

Collect all ingredients in a basin and stir with chopstick or handle of wooden spoon to avoid mashing. The mixture should not be too stiff or too runny. Season to taste. Garnish with chives and parsley or cress.

NOTE: Always include one or two crisp, crunchy foods in a rice salad, such as celery, nuts, peppers and fresh cucumber.

VARIATIONS:

Add to the Rice Salad:

50 g/2 oz raw, small mushrooms, chopped; 50 g/2 oz finely chopped green or red peppers; 6 stoned and chopped green or black olives, and 1 clove garlic, crushed with 1 level teaspoon salt.

25 g/1 oz finely chopped walnuts; 25 g/1 oz currants; 50 g/2 oz red or green pepper, seeds removed and finely chopped; 50 g/2 oz finely diced fresh cucumber.

Cooked cold peas; diced cooked carrot; chopped almonds, or chopped fennel.

Instead of mayonnaise and cream, mix in 2–3 tablespoons oil and vinegar or lemon juice to taste.

Potato Salad

METRIC/IMPERIAL

750 g/1½ lb potatoes
1 tablespoon oil
1 tablespoon vinegar
1 small onion, finely chopped
2 tablespoons double cream
2 tablespoons salad cream

1 tablespoon parsley or chives,
  chopped
1 level teaspoon salt
freshly ground pepper to taste
few sprigs cress or watercress

Boil potatoes in skins. Peel and dice. Mix together in salad bowl, oil, vinegar and salt and onion. Add potatoes and mix well.

When cool, stir in cream, salad cream, parsley or chives, pepper and more salt if needed. Garnish with cress or watercress. Serve with a green salad, nutmeats and hard-boiled eggs.

Serves 4

VARIATION: Stir in 2 level teaspoons caraway seeds instead of parsley. Add 2 tablespoons finely chopped red pepper. Stir in 1 chopped pickled cucumber.

Banana and Rice Salad with Curry Dressing

METRIC/IMPERIAL

50–75 g/2–3 oz red or green pepper, seeded and very thinly sliced
1 small onion, finely chopped
2 bananas, peeled and diced
4 heaped tablespoons cold, boiled rice
2 heaped tablespoons coarsely desiccated coconut

2 level teaspoons sugar
½ level teaspoon salt
1 level teaspoon curry powder or paste
2 tablespoons lemon juice
3–4 tablespoons oil
few sprigs watercress or cress
1 lemon twist

Combine pepper with onion, bananas, rice and coconut in a salad bowl.

Collect in a screw-top jar, sugar, salt, curry powder or paste, lemon juice and oil. Shake well, pour over salad and mix well with two forks or chopsticks. Garnish with cress or watercress and lemon twist.

Serves 4

VARIATION: Use chopped blanched almonds or walnuts instead of coconut.

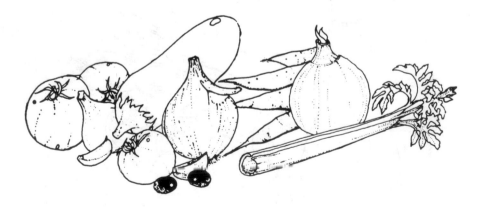

Peach or Pineapple Salad Plate

METRIC/IMPERIAL

125 g/4 oz cottage cheese
50 g/2 oz unsalted butter,
  softened
2 sticks celery, finely chopped
50 g/2 oz walnuts, chopped
pinch curry powder
1 medium-sized orange,
  seedless or with seeds
  removed

1 large lettuce
8 peach halves or pineapple
  rings
few sprigs watercress
2 tablespoons oil
2 tablespoons lemon juice
1 level teaspoon sugar

Mix together cheese, butter, celery, walnuts and curry powder. Grate orange rind. Peel orange with stainless steel knife and cut into 16 wedges.

Arrange on four plates, lettuce leaves, peach halves filled with cheese mix and topped with walnuts, orange wedges and watercress. Chill for 30 minutes–1 hour.

Shake together in screw-top jar orange rind, oil, lemon juice and sugar. Pour over salad plates just before serving.

Serves 4

Avocado Salad Plate

METRIC/IMPERIAL

4 avocado pears, peeled, stoned, diced and drained
grated rind and juice of 1 large lemon
8 lettuce leaves
2 large tomatoes, skinned and sliced
1 leek, halved, washed and thinly sliced
1 red pepper, seeded and cut into rings
bunch of watercress
1 tablespoon oil
1 tablespoon mayonnaise or salad cream
1 teaspoon sugar
salt to taste

Arrange in a pile on each plate, lettuce leaves, tomatoes, avocados, leek and red pepper. Surround with watercress.

Shake together in bottle, lemon juice, rind, oil, salad cream or mayonnaise, sugar and salt. Pour over piled salads. Serve with brown bread and butter.

Serves 4

NOTE: Diced avocado will keep fresh green colour if immediately put in bowl with lemon juice.

Banana Salad Plate

METRIC/IMPERIAL

4 large ripe bananas, peeled and halved
1 tablespoon lemon juice
heart of cos lettuce
50 g/2 oz salted peanuts or cashew nuts
4 tablespoons Curry Mayonnaise (see page 199)
few orange twists
pinch paprika
little cress

Arrange bananas in long cos lettuce leaves on four plates. Squeeze little lemon juice on the bananas. Using a spoon, coat bananas with curry mayonnaise. Sprinkle with chopped salted nuts and with paprika at each end. Garnish with orange twists and cress.

Serves 4

Fruit Salad Plate with Cheese

METRIC/IMPERIAL

50 g/2 oz Danish Blue cheese
50 g/2 oz cottage cheese
25 g/1 oz unsalted butter
little cream or top of milk
few drops green colouring
4 ripe pears, peeled, halved
   and cored
1 tablespoon olive oil

2 teaspoons lemon juice
sugar, salt and pepper to taste
8 lettuce leaves
1 small orange, cut in sections
few sprigs watercress
few black grapes or strip red
   pepper

Cream blue cheese, cottage cheese and softened butter together, adding a little cream if not quite soft enough. Dip a skewer into the green colouring and stir into the mixture. Pile up the centres of pears with cheese mixture. In a screw-top jar, shake the oil, lemon juice and seasonings.

Arrange the lettuce leaves, stems to centre on a dish. Place a pear half on each leaf. Pour a little dressing over the pear. Arrange orange sections between the pears, and sprigs of watercress, grapes or red pepper round the edge of the dish.

Serves 4

Iced Cheese Salad Plate

METRIC/IMPERIAL

125 g/4 oz cottage cheese
1 tablespoon melted butter
75 ml/⅛ pint evaporated milk
25 g/1 oz gherkins, chopped

1 tablespoon chopped fresh
   parsley and thyme
few lettuce leaves
few sliced tomatoes

Blend cheese, butter and milk to a smooth mixture. Stir in gherkins and herbs. Put in ice-tray and freeze until firm.

Cut in slices and arrange on lettuce leaves. Garnish with tomato slices. Serve with mayonnaise and crispbread or toast.

Serves 2–3

Greek Salad

METRIC/IMPERIAL

1 large lemon

½ clove garlic, crushed with
    ½ level teaspoon salt

2 tablespoons olive oil

black pepper, freshly ground

1 x 15-cm/6-inch piece
    cucumber, peeled, cut into
    5-mm/¼-inch slices, and
    then quarters

1 medium-sized onion, peeled
    and thinly sliced

125 g/4 oz small tomatoes,
    skinned and quartered

125 g/4 oz red and green
    peppers, seeded, and thinly
    sliced

125 g/4 oz black olives, stoned

2 hard-boiled eggs, cut into
    quarters

Grate lemon rind coarsely. Peel lemon with saw-edged, stainless steel knife. Then dice.

Crush garlic with salt in salad bowl. Mix with olive oil and freshly ground pepper. Add vegetables, olives, eggs and mix well. Sprinkle prepared lemon rind on top.

Serves 4

VARIATION: Mix 50–75 g/1–2 oz. Danish Blue with the cottage cheese and a little salt. Add some fresh marjoram.

Moroccan Salad

METRIC/IMPERIAL

75 g/3 oz onion, thinly sliced

1 medium-sized diced
    seedless, thin-skinned
    lemon

25 g/1 oz parsley, roughly
    chopped

2 teaspoons sugar

2 tablespoons olive oil

Mix all ingredients thoroughly together. Chill. Serve with cheese, crisp rolls or brown bread and butter.

Serves 4

NOTE: If using thick-skinned lemon, grate lemon rind on medium grater. Then peel lemon with a stainless saw-edged knife and chop.

Arabian Salad

METRIC/IMPERIAL

250 g/8 oz tomatoes, skinned
and sliced
1 or 2 medium-sized oranges,
peeled, seeds removed
1 small onion, thinly sliced
2 tablespoons olive oil

1 tablespoon lemon juice or
white vinegar
pinch of salt
little freshly grated black pepper
black olives, stoned
few chives, or green onion top

Cut orange peel into thin matchsticks. Slice flesh thinly. In a shallow serving dish, arrange overlapping slices of tomato and orange, with onion rings on top.

Shake together in a small screw-top jar, oil, lemon juice or vinegar and seasonings. Pour over the salad. Chill. Garnish with black olives and chives.

Serves 4

Nutty Salad

METRIC/IMPERIAL

½ level teaspoon salt
2 tablespoons oil
2 tablespoons lemon juice
1 teaspoon honey
1 teaspoon fresh ginger, finely
chopped or ½ level teaspoon
ground ginger

125–175 g/4–6 oz mushrooms,
washed and thinly sliced
50 g/2 oz walnuts, milled or
grated
little watercress

In a screw-top jar, shake together salt, oil, lemon juice, honey and ginger.

In salad bowl collect mushrooms and walnuts. Pour in salad dressing and mix well. Pile up in centre of bowl. Garnish edges with watercress.

Serves 4

Creamy Salad Dressing

METRIC/IMPERIAL
150 ml/¼ pint double cream
1 level teaspoon sugar
grated rind and juice of 1 small
  lemon

Mix all ingredients together in a basin, adding sugar and
lemon rind to taste. Add a little water if needed. This salad
dressing is good with cabbage and lettuce.

Serves 4

Blue Cheese Dressing 1 (strong flavour)

METRIC/IMPERIAL
150 ml/¼ pint olive oil
150 ml/¼ pint vinegar or lemon
  juice or mixed
1 tablespoon sugar

1 teaspoon salt
125 g/4 oz fresh Danish Blue
  cheese, crumbled
ground black pepper

Collect all ingredients in blender goblet and liquidize. Thin
down with a little water if liked. Alternatively, collect all
ingredients in a large screw-top jar and shake well to mix.
Store in a cool place.

Serves 4

Blue Cheese Dressing 2 (creamy, mild flavour)

METRIC/IMPERIAL

4 tablespoons salad cream or
  mayonnaise
1 tablespoon oil
25 g/1 oz Danish Blue cheese,
  crumbled

1 tablespoon milk
1 drop green colouring

Method as for Blue Cheese Dressing 1.

Serves 4

Blue Cheese Dressing 3 (creamy, rich strong flavour)

METRIC/IMPERIAL

6 tablespoons mayonnaise
1 tablespoon tomato sauce
50 g/2 oz Danish Blue cheese,
  crumbled

1 tablespoon milk
2 teaspoons lemon juice or
  vinegar

Method as for Blue Cheese Dressing 1.

Serves 4

Creamy Tomato Dressing

METRIC/IMPERIAL

tomato sauce to taste
double cream to taste
evaporated milk to taste
4 tablespoons bottled salad
  cream

Mix all ingredients together.

Serves 4

Tangy Tomato Dressing

METRIC/IMPERIAL
2 tablespoons tomato sauce
Worcestershire sauce to taste
4 tablespoons salad cream
dash Tabasco

Mix all ingredients together.

Serves 2–3

Thousand Island Dressing

METRIC/IMPERIAL
150 ml/¼ pint salad cream
1 tablespoon onion, finely
  chopped
1 tablespoon red pepper, finely
  chopped
1 tablespoon gherkin or pickled
  cucumber, finely chopped

1 tablespoon stoned black or
  green olives, finely chopped
little finely chopped parsley or
  chives

Mix all ingredients together.

Serves 4

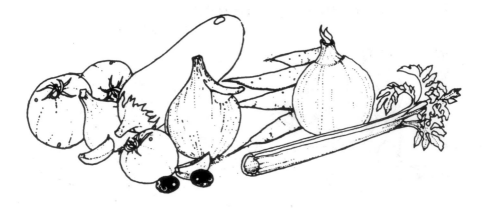

Mayonnaise

METRIC/IMPERIAL

2 egg yolks
½ level teaspoon salt
150 ml/¼ pint oil

½–1 tablespoon lemon juice or
vinegar

Method 1

In a blender, blend egg yolks, salt and lemon for 2 seconds.
Add oil slowly, at low speed.

Method 2

Whisk egg yolks and salt in a mixing bowl. Add oil by
teaspoonfuls. When mixture becomes thicker, pour oil in a thin
trickle, whisking steadily. The mixture should be a thick
cream. Stir in lemon juice to taste.

Store in a wide-mouthed jar with tight lid. Keep in cool
place.

Serves 4–5

VARIATIONS: Mix in grated orange or lemon rind.

Add a pinch of curry powder and a shake of garlic salt gives a different
tang.

Stir in chopped gherkins, olives, red peppers, finely chopped onion.

Stir in chopped fresh parsley, thyme, chives, and grated lemon rind. This
is good with green salads.

For foamy mayonnaise, stir into the mayonnaise a tablespoon of single
cream. Fold in stiffly beaten egg whites, using a silver spoon. Serve in bowl
with a spoon. This is also good with green salads.

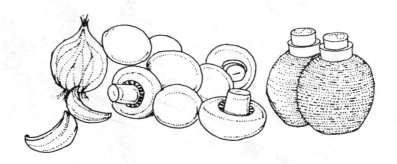

Curry Mayonnaise

METRIC/IMPERIAL

1 small onion, finely chopped
15 g/½ oz margarine and
1 level tablespoon curry
powder
150 ml/¼ pint salad cream or
mayonnaise

2 tablespoons double cream or
2 teaspoons almond or
cashew nut cream blended
with 1 tablespoon warm
water
squeeze lemon juice

Fry onion in margarine until pale yellow. Add curry powder and cook 1–2 minutes. Rub through a strainer to make paste.

Combine curry paste with salad cream or mayonnaise. Stir in cream and add lemon juice to taste.

Serves 4

Peanut Salad Cream

METRIC/IMPERIAL

2 rounded tablespoons
smooth peanut butter
1 tablespoon vegetable oil
1–2 tablespoons lemon juice or
vinegar

1 level teaspoon curry powder
1 level teaspoon sugar
3–4 tablespoons water

Work well together in a bowl with a wooden spoon, peanut butter, oil, lemon juice or vinegar, curry powder and sugar. Stir in water to make a cream. Beat well.

This dressing is good with cabbage salads.

Serves 4

VARIATION: Flavour this salad cream with grated lemon and orange rind.

Hungarian Salad Dressing

METRIC/IMPERIAL

1 carton natural unsweetened
   yogurt
1 level teaspoon paprika
1 tablespoon double cream
1 tablespoon bottled tomato
   sauce

garlic salt to taste or 1 level
   teaspoon onion
   soup mix, or finely chopped
   onion

Collect all ingredients in a screw-top jar and shake to mix.
Chill until required.

Serves 3

Herb Dressing

METRIC/IMPERIAL

1 carton natural unsweetened
   yogurt
2 tablespoons evaporated milk
1 teaspoon vegetable oil
1 tablespoon lemon juice
1 tablespoon chopped chives

1 tablespoon chopped parsley
½ tablespoon chopped thyme
little grated lemon rind
salt and pepper to taste

Collect all ingredients in a screw-top jar and shake to mix.
Chill until required.

Serves 3

Breads

White Bread

METRIC/IMPERIAL

300 ml/½ pint warm water
1 teaspoon sugar or honey
25 g/1 oz fresh yeast or 1 level
  tablespoon dried yeast

3 cups flour (300 ml/½ pint
  size)
2 level teaspoons salt

Put water, sugar or honey, yeast (if using dried yeast, mix with the sugar first of all then add warm water) and one cup of the flour into a mixing bowl. Mix to a batter and leave in a warm place for 10 minutes.

Tip in remaining flour and salt all at once. Mix to a soft dough with the hand, then squeeze and work it until it leaves the bowl clean. Pull and stretch dough on an unfloured board, about 50 times until it feels firm and less sticky,

Put dough into a covered oiled saucepan, closed casserole or polythene bag closed with a rubber band. Leave to stand in a warm place until it doubles in size.

Turn onto an oiled or lightly floured table. Flatten and roll up like a Swiss roll. Repeat once or twice until dough feels springy.

Shape into rolls or a loaf (see pages 206 and 207). Place on floured tray, brush tops with oil, put inside a polythene bag. Stand in a warm place to swell again, about 10-15 minutes. This is called proving.

Bake in a preheated hot oven (200°C/400°F, Gas Mark 6), rolls on top shelf, loaf on middle shelf, until they are brown on base and on top, and feel light in the hand (30 minutes for rolls and 45–50 minutes for loaf). Cool on a rack.

Makes 625–750 g/1¼–1½ lb loaf or 16 rolls

VARIATIONS:
Flower Pot Loaf: Older people know that bread baked in brick ovens, with solid heat, had a fine flavour and texture, because it was baked right through. The same effect can be obtained by baking bread in a brick flower pot. It will take longer, but it is the safest and best way of baking bread. The brick pot ensures a steady solid heat and prevents burning. Instead of loaf tins, use 10-cm/4-inch or 12-cm/5-inch pots, washed, dried, thickly greased with hard fat, or oil and coated inside with cornflakes or wheatgerm. Bake 1–1¼ hours.

Quick Bread: Press dough, 5 cm/2 inches thick, into a greased Yorkshire tin. Brush top with milk mixed with oil, dredge with flour or sprinkle with crushed cornflakes. Let rise inside a polythene bag. Bake in usual way. Cut in squares when cool.

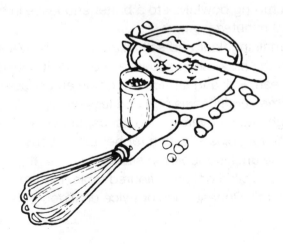

Vita Bread

METRIC/IMPERIAL

300 ml/½ pint warm water
1 teaspoon sugar
25 g/1 oz fresh yeast or 1 level
   tablespoon dried yeast
625 g/1¼ lb strong plain white
   flour
50 g/2 oz wheatgerm
2 rounded tablespoons dried,
   skimmed milk (40 g/1½ oz)

1 egg or 25 g/1 oz soya flour
1–2 level tablespoons yeast
   powder (5 g/¼ oz)
2 level teaspoons salt
little salted water, or a
   teaspoon oil mixed with 1
   teaspoon milk

Mix water, sugar, yeast (if using fresh yeast mix with sugar first then add water, etc), and one-third of the flour. Stir to a batter. Leave to stand in a warm place for 15 minutes until frothy.

Tip in remaining ingredients all at once, reserving a little of the wheatgerm. Mix with hands, adding more water if necessary, until there is no dry flour left in the bowl.

Make a soft dough by squeezing and working with the hand. This dough is rather sticky because of the dried milk. Pull and stretch the dough on an unfloured board about 30–40 times until it feels firmer.

Lightly dust board with the remaining wheatgerm. Divide dough into two pieces, flatten each dough piece and roll up like a Swiss roll. Place rolls in a greased loaf tin, brush tops with oil.

Put inside a polythene bag and leave until risen to top of the tin. For a crisp crust, brush with salted water. For a soft crust, brush with mixture of oil and milk and dredge with flour.

Bake for 45–50 minutes on middle shelf of a preheated hot oven (200°C/400°F/Gas Mark 6). It is done when it looks brown, feels light in the hand and is loose in the tin.

Makes two 500 g/1 lb loaves

NOTE: The bread has so much food value that just 3 or 4 slices of it provide a large proportion of the recommended intakes of vitamin B, iron, calcium and protein for adults.

Tomato Bread

METRIC/IMPERIAL

300 ml/½ pint warm water
1 teaspoon sugar
25 g/1 oz fresh yeast or 1 level
   tablespoon dried yeast

1 egg
375 g/12 oz plain white flour
1 packet tomato soup mix
little paprika for the top

Mix water, sugar, yeast (if using dried yeast first mix with sugar then add the warm water), egg and 125 g/4 oz flour. Stir to a batter. Leave to stand 15-20 minutes or 10 minutes if in a warm place.

Tip in remaining flour and soup mix. Mix to a dough with the hand. Add more water to take up any dry flour if necessary, then squeeze and work to make a soft dough. Knead the dough on an unfloured board about 50 times until it feels firm and no longer sticky.

Flatten dough and roll up like a Swiss roll. Place roll in a greased loaf tin. Brush top with oil and put inside a polythene bag. Leave to rise to top of the tin. Spray or brush the top with salted water. Bake on middle shelf of a preheated hot oven (200°C/400°F, Gas Mark 6), until loose in the tin (about 20 minutes for rolls or 50 minutes for loaf) – the bread should sound hollow when tapped on the base.

Cool on a rack, brush hot loaf with water and sprinkle paprika over top.

Makes 750 g/1½ lb loaf or 20 rolls

VARIATIONS: Make other savoury loaves for salad meals, using mushroom, celery, leek or onion soup powders. Remember to omit salt.

Herb Bread

METRIC/IMPERIAL

300 ml/½ pint warm water
1 teaspoon sugar
25 g/1 oz fresh yeast or 1 level
   tablespoon dried yeast
375 g/12 oz plain white flour
150 ml/¼ pint boiling water

1 x 125 g/4 oz packet stuffing
   mix
1 egg or 25 g/1 oz soya flour
little oil
little salt water (3 teaspoons
   salt to 150 ml/¼ pint water)

Mix 150 ml/¼ pint warm water, sugar, yeast (if using dried yeast, first mix with sugar then add the warm water), and 125 g/4 oz of the flour, stir to a batter and stand in a warm place for about 15 minutes.

Put stuffing into a bowl and pour over the boiling water. Add this to the liquid mixture with the remaining flour, and the egg or soya flour. Mix with the hand, adding a little more water to take up any dry flour, or a little more flour if too wet.

Make a soft dough by squeezing and working with the hand, knead thoroughly by pulling and stretching it about 50 times on an unfloured board, until it feels elastic and no longer sticky. Dust lightly with flour, flatten and roll like a Swiss roll.

Place roll in two 500-g/1-lb oiled loaf tins, brush tops with oil. Put inside polythene bags and leave until risen to double size. Brush top with salt water. Bake on middle shelf of a preheated hot oven (200°C/400°F, Gas Mark 6) for about 40–50 minutes. Cool on a rack, or standing on end in the tin.

Makes two 500 g/1 lb loaves

VARIATIONS: Press half herb dough into a greased Yorkshire pudding tin, 25 x 18 x 7 cm/10 x 7 x 3 inches approx. Leave to rise as before. Before baking, top with 75 g/3 oz soft cheese, coarsely grated, and dusted with flour
   Add 1 teaspoon grated lemon rind to dough mix.
   Use sage and onion mix. This goes well with Lancashire cheese.
   Use fresh, home-made stuffing of breadcrumbs, herbs, nut fat or hard margarine, lemon rind and onion.

Wheatmeal Loaf

METRIC/IMPERIAL

25 g/1 oz fresh yeast or 1 level
  tablespoon dried yeast
1 teaspoon honey or sugar
1 cup warm water
1 egg, unbeaten or 1 heaped
  tablespoon soya flour

salted water (2 teaspoons salt
  to 150 ml/¼ pint water)
2 cups plain flour
1 cup wholemeal flour
2 level teaspoons salt
little oil

If using fresh yeast, first mix with honey or sugar then add the warm water and the egg or soya flour. If using dried yeast, mix the first four ingredients together and then allow to stand for 5–10 minutes.

Tip the flour and salt on to the liquid mixture all at once. Mix together with one hand, adding more water if any dry flour remains. Add a little more flour if the mixture is too wet.

Work ingredients together to make a soft, but firm dough (like scones), wiping it round the bowl. When dough leaves the basin clean it is ready. Knead the dough on an unfloured board, until it feels elastic and less sticky. Lightly dust with flour and shape into a ball or roll.

Divide into four pieces. Shape each piece to a large round roll. Place rolls in a row in a greased 1-kg/2-lb loaf tin. Brush with oil. Place inside a polythene bag. Leave to rise in a warm place until doubled in size.

Spray or brush the top with salt and water and sprinkle with flour. Bake on middle shelf of a preheated hot oven (200°C/400°F, Gas Mark 6), for about 50 minutes.

The loaf is done when it looks brown, shrinks a little from the sides of the tin and feels light in the hand. It should sound hollow when tapped on the base.

Makes 625–750 g/1¼–1½ lb loaf

VARIATION: Another way of making the loaf is to shape the dough to an 18-cm/7-inch roll and place in the tin to rise. Make three slits on the top before baking.

Wheatmeal Rolls

METRIC/IMPERIAL
Ingredients are same as for Wheatmeal Loaf, opposite.

Follow method for Wheatmeal Loaf, opposite, until the dough is ready to use.

Cut into 12 or 16 pieces (approx. 40–50 g/1½–2 oz). Roll each piece to a ball on an unfloured board or table top, using the palm of the hand. Press hard down at first, then ease up, cupping your fingers right round the dough piece and roll lightly.

Put rolls on a floured baking tray. For soft-sided rolls, place 1 cm/½ inch apart. Brush tops with oil. Put tray inside a large polythene bag. Leave on table until puffed up and doubled in size. This may take 45 minutes–1 hour.

Spray or brush with salted water. Bake on top shelf in a preheated hot oven (200°C/400°F, Gas Mark 6) for about 25–30 minutes until they are brown on top and bottom, and feel light in the hand. Cool on a rack.

Makes 12–16 rolls

Garlic Bread

METRIC/IMPERIAL
2–4 cloves garlic
½ level teaspoon salt
75–125 g/3–4 oz butter or
  margarine

500 g/1 lb loaf preferably
  Vienna or French stick

Crush garlic with salt on a board, using the flat of a knife, or in a salad bowl with a wooden spoon. Work in butter or margarine.

Slice loaf nearly through. Spread each slice with garlic butter. Wrap in foil and put on a baking tin. Bake on top shelf in preheated hot oven (200°C/400°F, Gas Mark 6), for about 10–15 minutes. Serve hot.

Serves 4

Coconut Rolls

METRIC/IMPERIAL

1 cup warm water
3 teaspoons sugar
25 g/1 oz fresh yeast or 1 level
    tablespoon dried yeast
3 cups flour
1 cup plus 50 g/2 oz
    desiccated coconut

1 egg or 25 g/1 oz soya flour
2 level teaspoons salt
little salted water (2 rounded
    teaspoons to 300 ml/½ pint)

Mix water, sugar, yeast (if using dried yeast, mix with sugar first then add the warm water) and one-third of the flour. Stir to a batter then leave in a warm place for 10 minutes.

Add remaining flour, 1 cup of coconut, egg or soya flour and salt. Mix to a soft dough with your hands.

Pull and stretch the dough on an unfloured board (about 50 times) until it feels firm and less sticky.

Cut kneaded dough into four and then each piece in up to eight. Roll each piece of dough into a ball on an unfloured table, using the palm of the hand. Press down hard at first, then ease off, cupping fingers round the ball and roll lightly.

Dip each roll in salted water, then in remaining coconut. Pack on a floured tray 1 cm/½ inch apart. Put in a polythene bag, leave on table to rise and double in size.

Bake on top shelf of a preheated hot oven (200°C/400°F, Gas Mark 6) for 15–20 minutes.

Makes 25–30 small rolls

VARIATION:
Sweet Coconut Loaf: Add 25 g/1 oz sugar to dry mix. Brush top of hot loaf, when baked, with a wet brush dipped in honey or syrup.

Bread and Butter Rusks

METRIC/IMPERIAL
500 g/1 lb bread, sliced
50–75 g/2–3 oz butter or
    margarine

Butter bread. Place in baking tin. Bake on middle shelf in very cool oven (120°C/265°F, Gas Mark ½), for 1–1½ hours, until light brown and crisp. Store in a tin.

Serves 4–5

VARIATION:
Savoury Rusks: Add to 75 g/3 oz margarine, 50 g/2 oz finely grated cheese or 1 teaspoon yeast extractfor 2 teaspoons curry powder.

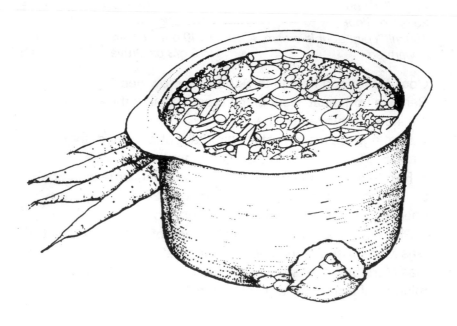

Light Meals and Snacks

Soufflé aux Blancs d'Oeufs

METRIC/IMPERIAL

40 g/1½ oz butter
25 g/1 oz flour
150 ml/¼ pint double cream,
  warmed

salt, pepper and nutmeg to taste
6–7 egg whites
140 g/4½ oz Gruyère, grated
75 g/3 oz Gruyère, diced small

Cook butter and flour in thick pan over low heat until foamy. Remove from heat. Beat in the cream. Boil to thicken for 1 minute. Remove from heat.

Beat egg whites until stiff. Stir in about one-third, together with 75 g/3 oz grated cheese, then the diced cheese.

Fold in remaining egg whites. Put into one large dish or six small dishes buttered and sprinkled with 25 g/1 oz grated cheese. Sprinkle remaining cheese on top.

Place on middle shelf of a preheated hot oven (200°C/400°F, Gas Mark 6) and reduce heat to moderately hot (190°C/375°F, Gas Mark 5). Bake until puffed and brown, for about 20–25 minutes, if using one large dish and 15 minutes if using the six small ones.

Serves 4

NOTE: Egg whites will keep in the freezer part of refrigerator for 2 weeks.

Hot Cheese Soufflé

METRIC/IMPERIAL

50 g/2 oz butter
1 tablespoon breadcrumbs
*   and grated cheese, mixed*
125 g/4 oz dry cheese, grated
50 g/2 oz flour
1 level teaspoon salt

300 ml/½ pint hot milk
¼ level teaspoon pepper
4 eggs, separated
pinch cayenne pepper and
*   grated nutmeg*

Butter 1.2-litre/3-pint ovenproof dish or four individual dishes and sprinkle with breadcrumbs and cheese.

Break eggs, putting whites in a large clean mixing bowl or preferably a copper bowl. Melt flour and butter together in thick pan over low heat until frothy. Remove from heat. Gradually beat in milk, using a wooden spoon or whisk. Cook over low heat, stirring well until the sauce is smooth and thick.

Beat egg yolks until thick and pale yellow. Add to the sauce and beat well. Stir in remaining cheese and seasonings. Cool to lukewarm. Beat egg whites into peaks with a balloon or rotary whisk. Stir 2 tablespoons into the cheese mixture. Fold in the rest lightly and quickly using a metal tablespoon.

Fill prepared dish or dishes three-quarters full. Make a slight depression in the centre with a spoon. Bake on middle shelf of preheated hot oven (200°C/400°F, Gas Mark 6), for 25 minutes. It is done when brown and firm to the touch in the centre or when a knitting needle comes out clean.

Serve in the dish in which it is cooked, wrapped in a folded napkin, standing on a flat meat dish for handling.

Serves 4

NOTE: The soufflé mixture can be prepared beforehand, up to the stage of adding the egg whites and kept just warm. After folding in the whites it must be baked at once or, after the soufflé mould has been filled, it can be covered with a big warmed basin or saucepan to protect it from draughts and then baked as convenient up to 45 minutes later.

Soufflés can be baked at 160°C/325°F standing in a tin of hot water. After the soufflé has risen, increase the heat to 200°C/400°F to brown.

American Cheese Soufflé

METRIC/IMPERIAL

125–175 g/4–6 oz fresh brown
 or white breadcrumbs
125–175 g/4–6 oz strong
 cheese, grated
1 teaspoon salt mixed with
 ½ teaspoon pepper and
 ½ teaspoon dry mustard

2 eggs, beaten
2 eggs, separated
450 ml/¾ pint hot milk
150 ml/¼ pint single cream

Mix breadcrumbs, cheese and seasonings and put in a greased 1.2-litre/2-pint dish or small dishes.

Mix together eggs, 1 yolk, milk and cream. Fold in 2 whites, stiffly beaten. Pour crumbs and cheese on top.

Stand dish in a pan of hot water. Bake on middle shelf of a moderately hot oven (190°C/375°F, Gas Mark 5) for 30–40 minutes, until puffed and set. Increase heat to 200°C/400°F, Gas Mark 6 to brown the top. Serve at once.

Serves 4

VARIATION: For stronger flavour, use 50 g/2 oz Danish Blue and 125 g/4 oz Cheddar. Use 1 teaspoon French mustard, mixed with eggs and milk, instead of dry mustard.

Cold Cheese Soufflé

2 level teaspoons Gelozone
1 tablespoon cold water
300 ml/½ pint water
1 teaspoon savoury extract
2 teaspoons white vinegar
125 g/4 oz Gruyère cheese,
    grated
50 g/2 oz Parmesan cheese,
    grated

pinch salt, pepper and
    cayenne pepper
1 level teaspoon French
    mustard
300 ml/½ pint double cream,
    whipped
few stuffed olives, sliced or
    pinch paprika

Mix Gelozone to a paste with cold water. Add remaining water. Boil for 1 minute. Then cool in a bowl.

Stir in savoury extract and vinegar. Whisk until frothy and nearly set. Stir in cheese, mixed with seasonings and mustard. Fold in cream, using a silver spoon. Fill into small china soufflé dishes or paper cases. Chill to set.

Garnish each soufflé with olives or paprika. Serve with thin dry toast.

Serves 4

VARIATION:
Cold Cheese Soufflé Danoise: Use 300 ml/½ pint water less 2 tablespoons. Use 125 g/4 oz crumbled Danish Blue, and 125 g/4 oz grated mild Cheddar, instead of Gruyère and Parmesan. Omit vinegar, mustard and cayenne pepper. Stir in 2 tablespoons dry sherry and squeeze lemon juice with the savoury extract.

Yogurt Curd Cheese

METRIC/IMPERIAL

600 ml/1 pint natural yogurt   *little double cream, if liked*
1 teaspoon salt

Stand a bowl of yogurt in hot water to warm. This should make
it curdle. Pour through a square of muslin, draped over a nylon
strainer and place over a basin. Leave to drip. Gather up the
four corners. Tie firmly with string, like a pudding. Press in a
bowl with a saucer of weights on top. When it is firm it is ready.

   Mash with a little more salt and the cream if liked.

Serves 4

NOTE: Yogurt is the perfect accompaniment to curries. It clears the palate
and balances the meal by adding calcium, good quality protein and vitamins
A and B.

Oriental Cream Cheese

METRIC/IMPERIAL

50–75 g/2–3 oz sultanas   *sugar to taste*
4 bananas (ripe, but not brown)   *salt to taste*
1 lemon   *50 g/2 oz salted nuts*
500 g/1 lb cream cheese or   *little cress*
   375 g/12 oz cottage or curd   *few lemon slices*
   cheese and 150 ml/¼ pint   *few black olives or Pickled*
   double cream   *Prunes (see pages 172)*
2 level teaspoons curry powder

Cook sultanas in 4 tablespoons water, over low heat, to make
them juicy.

   Slice and chop bananas with juice of ½ lemon in a basin.

   Blend cheese, cream and curry powder. Mix in sultanas
and banana with lemon. Add sugar, salt and little grated
lemon rind. Serve on a pottery dish, roughen surface with two
forks and sprinkle with salted nuts. Top with a lemon twist and
surround with cress and black olives or pickled prunes.

Serves 4

Avocado Cream Cheese

METRIC/IMPERIAL

125 g/4 oz cottage cheese
150 ml/¼ pint double cream
2 hard-boiled eggs
1 small onion, finely chopped
1 tablespoon mayonnaise
2 avocado pears, halved and
  stoned
½ level teaspoon freshly
  ground black pepper

1 level teaspoon salt
1 teaspoon lemon juice
little cress
few lemon twists
few thin strips red pepper,
  blanched or canned pepper

Press cottage cheese through a wire strainer, to make it smooth, into large bowl. Add cream, chopped egg, onion and mayonnaise. Blend together.

Scrape out the pale green flesh from avocados, with a silver or plastic spoon, close to the skin. Blend with the cream cheese mixture. Add freshly ground black pepper, salt and lemon juice.

Chill. Serve on a pottery dish, roughen surface with two forks, and garnish with cress and lemon twists and red pepper.

Garlic Cheese

METRIC/IMPERIAL

1–2 tablespoons chopped
  parsley
1 level teaspoon sea salt
2 cloves garlic

125 g/4 oz cottage cheese
25 g/1 oz unsalted butter,
  softened

In a pestle and mortar, pound together parsley, salt and garlic. Work in cheese and butter to make a smooth paste. Shape to a flat round on oiled board, with oiled hands. Wrap in foil and chill. Serve with toast or crispbread.

Serves 4

Potted Cheese

METRIC/IMPERIAL

500 g/1 lb cheese, grated
coarsely
1 tablespoon savoury extract

1 large can evaporated milk

Melt cheese, savoury extract and milk together in a china bowl in a saucepan of warm water over lowest possible heat. The water must never be more than hand hot or the mixture will be tough and stringy.

When melted, add one of the following flavourings and pour into one large or several small pots such as soufflé dishes or pottery egg cups. The cheeses can be turned out or served in the pots.

Serves 8

Each of the following flavourings is for one-quarter of the total recipe quantity:

Onion Cheese: Add 4 tablespoons onion soup mix or 4 tablespoons chopped onion, fried in butter.

Sage Cheese: Add finely chopped fresh or dried sage to taste.

Tomato Cheese: Add 4 tablespoons tomato purée and a shake Worcester sauce.

Walnut Cheese: Add 25 g/1 oz chopped walnuts and pinch curry powder.

Almond Cheese: Add 25 g/1 oz chopped almonds and 25 g/1 oz Tartex.

Herb Cheese: Add chopped fresh parsley, thyme and marjoram or dried mixed herbs to taste.

Caraway Cheese: Add 2 teaspoons caraway seeds and 1 teaspoon paprika.

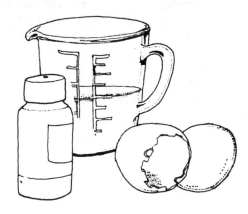

Pot Kase

METRIC/IMPERIAL

500 g/1 lb cheese, grated
  finely
50 g/2 oz softened butter
pinch cayenne pepper
1 level teaspoon ground mace
  or nutmeg

150 ml/¼ pint sweet sherry,
  port or dry sherry and
  ½ teaspoon sugar
50 g/2 oz melted butter or
  margarine

Work all ingredients together with a wooden spoon or fork to make a stiff paste. Fill small pots with the mixture and cover with butter or margarine. Store in refrigerator.

Serves 4

Welsh Rarebit

METRIC/IMPERIAL

250 g/8 oz strong Cheddar or
  Cheshire cheese, grated
25 g/1 oz butter
150 ml/¼ pint stout or strong
  ale

1 level teaspoon dry mustard
½ teaspoon paprika
2 egg yolks

Melt cheese and butter slowly in double boiler over hot water. When half melted, stir in the ale slowly. Sprinkle in mustard and paprika. Stir in egg yolks and warm through.

Pour over slices of hot, dry toast. Brown quickly under hot grill. Serve at once.

Serves 4

Camembert Croquettes

METRIC/IMPERIAL

40 g/1½ oz butter
40 g/1½ oz flour
300 ml/½ pint milk
1 Camembert cheese
   (175 g/ 6 oz)
1 egg yolk
salt, pepper and cayenne
   pepper to taste

little beaten egg
white breadcrumbs or
   wheatgerm
oil for frying (about 1 cm/
   ½ inch deep)
little chopped parsley

Melt butter and flour together. Stir in milk. Boil to thicken. Cool.

Remove most of the rind from the Camembert and press cheese through a wire sieve.

Add egg yolk and cheese to the milk mixture, and work to a stiff paste. Spread on a plate to cool.

Shape into walnut-sized pieces on a floured board. Brush with egg. Shake in bag with crumbs until completely coated. Fry in oil until brown, turning frequently. Drain on paper. Keep hot. Serve sprinkled with parsley.

Serves 4

VARIATION: Substitute Cheddar or Cheshire cheese for Camembert.

Iced Camembert

METRIC/IMPERIAL

50 g/2 oz unsalted butter, creamed

1 Camembert cheese (a not quite ripe one will do)

2 tablespoons dry sherry or white wine

salt and freshly ground black pepper to taste

dash cayenne pepper

50 g/2 oz fresh brown breadcrumbs or wheatgerm

few radishes

few celery curls

Remove most of the rind from the cheese and press through a coarse strainer or wire sieve.

Combine cheese, sherry or wine and butter and work to a stiff paste. Season. Remould mixture to its original shape on an oiled board. Coat thickly with breadcrumbs or wheatgerm. Wrap in foil or waxed paper. Freeze.

Serve, cut in wedges, on a wooden platter, garnished with radishes and celery.

Serves 6

VARIATION:

Iced Blue Cheese: Substitute 50 g/2 oz Danish Blue and 125 g/4 oz mild Cheddar or Caerphilly for Camembert. Omit sherry. Add 2 tablespoons double cream. Combine all ingredients to a smooth paste. Coat with parsley instead of breadcrumbs.

Bread Roast

METRIC/IMPERIAL

4 slices bread
50 g/2 oz butter
25 g/1 oz walnuts, crushed
125 g/4 oz strong cheese,
    grated

1–2 tablespoons dry sherry
1 level teaspoon yeast extract
1 level teaspoon curry powder
garlic salt to taste or clove of
    garlic, crushed with little salt

Gently fry bread in butter. Put into ovenproof dish and keep hot.

Combine walnuts, cheese, sherry, extract, seasonings and remaining melted butter from the frying pan. Work to make a smooth paste, using a wooden spoon. Spread on the fried bread and grill lightly.

Serves 4

Cheese d'Artois

METRIC/IMPERIAL

125 g/4 oz puff pastry
1 egg, beaten
50 g/2 oz Parmesan cheese,
    grated
75 g/3 oz dry Cheddar cheese,
    grated

salt, pepper and cayenne to
    taste
25 g/1 oz butter or margarine
few sprigs watercress

Roll pastry thinly to an oblong, 40 x 15 cms/16 x 6 inches. Divide in two, lengthwise.

Mix together egg, cheese, seasonings and butter, reserving a little egg for brushing. Spread mixture on one piece of pastry to within 1 cm/½ inch of edges. Wet edges. Place other half on top. Press together. Mark edges with a fork.

Brush with egg and water. Mark across in fingers with back of a knife. Bake on top shelf of very hot oven (230°C/450°F, Gas Mark 8), for 10–15 minutes or until brown. Serve hot, garnished with watercress.

Serves 4–5

Cheese Meringues

METRIC/IMPERIAL

2 egg whites, stiffly beaten to
  peaks
2 rounded tablespoons grated
  Parmesan cheese

pinch salt and cayenne pepper
oil for deep frying
little cress or parsley

Gently fold cheese into egg whites. Season.

Heat the oil to a temperature of 190°C/375°F.

Drop mixture into hot fat, a tablespoonful at a time. Fry for
2–3 minutes until they are golden brown. Remove with
perforated spoon and drain well on kitchen paper. Serve very
hot, garnished with cress or parsley.

Serves 4–5

Cheese Puffs

METRIC/IMPERIAL

16 x 5-cm/2-inch rounds or
  squares bread, about
  5 mm/¼ inch thick
50 g/2 oz butter or margarine,
  creamed
1 level teaspoon yeast extract

1 tablespoon tomato purée
75–125 g/3–4 oz cheese,
  grated
½ level teaspoon baking
  powder
1 egg, separated

Spread bread with mixture of butter, yeast extract and tomato
purée.

Mix together cheese, baking powder and egg yolk. Fold in
stiffly beaten white. Spread mixture on bread and bake on top
shelf of preheated hot oven (200°C/400°F, Gas Mark 6) for
15 minutes until brown. Serve hot or cold.

Serves 4

NOTE: They can be stored in a tin for a day or two.

Cheese Straws or Biscuits

METRIC/IMPERIAL

50 g/2 oz butter
50 g/2 oz flour
75 g/3 oz strong Cheddar or
   Cheshire cheese, grated
pinch cayenne pepper
½ teaspoon salt
1 teaspoon dry mustard

2 rounded teaspoons brewer's
   yeast powder or 1 level
   teaspoon yeast extract
   (optional)
1 egg yolk
1–2 tablespoons water

Lightly rub butter into flour. Add cheese, seasonings, mustard and yeast extract. Mix to a stiff paste with yolk and water, using a blunt knife or a fork.

Roll out thinly on floured board. Let stand 5 minutes.

Cut into 5-mm/¼-inch strips and into six rings, using two pastry cutters, 2.5-cm/1-inch size, and 1.5-cm/¾-inch size. Transfer to a floured baking sheet. Bake on top shelf of a preheated hot oven (200°C/400°F, Gas Mark 6) or under low grill for about 5–7 minutes.

Collect the straws into small bundles and place in the rings. Dust with paprika and serve hot.

Serves 4

NOTE: Cheese straws can be stored in an air-tight tin.

VARIATIONS: Omit salt. Substitute one level tablespoon tomato soup powder. Cut into small round biscuits and prick with a fork. Bake as before.

Omit mustard. Substitute 15 g/½ oz chopped walnuts and 1 level teaspoon curry powder. Cut into small squares or straws.

Tomato Ice

METRIC/IMPERIAL

150 ml/¼ pint rich mayonnaise
150 ml/¼ pint sour cream
150 ml/¼ tomato juice
1 level tablespoon tomato
  purée
1 small clove garlic, crushed
  with ½ level teaspoon salt

2 teaspoons onion soup mix
lemon juice
salt and pepper to taste
1 x 2.5-cm/1-inch piece
  cucumber, diced or sliced

Combine all ingredients, except cucumber. Season rather more than usual, as freezing reduces the flavour. Put the mixture in the ice-tray or in a dish in the freezing compartment. Stir occasionally.

Serve in glass cups, garnished with cucumber. Hand hot cheese biscuits or cheese straws separately.

Serves 4

NOTE: This recipe can also be used as an appetizer.

Chilaly

METRIC/IMPERIAL

1 teaspoon finely chopped
  onion
1 tablespoon finely chopped
  red pepper
25 g/1 oz butter
1 medium-sized tomato,
  skinned and pulped

375 g/12 oz cheese, grated
3 tablespoons milk
1 egg, beaten
salt and cayenne pepper to
  taste

Gently fry onion and pepper in butter for 5 minutes. Add tomato, cheese, milk and egg. Stir over low heat to make a thick mixture. Season. Serve hot, in small cocottes, with thin toast.

Serves 4

Mushrooms on Toast

METRIC/IMPERIAL

250 g/8 oz mushroom caps,
  sliced
½ small clove garlic, crushed
  with ½ level teaspoon salt
50 g/2 oz butter or margarine

150 ml/¼ pint stout
Worcestershire sauce to taste
salt to taste
cayenne pepper
4 pieces buttered toast

Cook mushroom caps with garlic and salt in butter in a
covered thick pan over low heat for 5 minutes. Add stout,
Worcestershire sauce and seasonings. Simmer for 10 minutes.
Then cook with lid off until liquid is reduced to about
1 tablespoon. Serve on toast, with liquid poured round.

Serves 4

Danish Prunes

METRIC/IMPERIAL

250 g/8 oz large prunes
  (8–12 prunes)
150 ml/¼ pint sweet red wine
150 ml/¼ pint water
125 g/4 oz Danish Blue cheese

50 g/2 oz unsalted butter
1 teaspoon savoury extract
75 g/3 oz salted almonds
few sprigs watercress

Soak prunes overnight in wine and water in a covered
saucepan. Simmer in the pan over low heat for about
20 minutes or until all the liquid is absorbed. Cool and stone.
  Mash cheese, butter and savoury extract together. Stuff the
prunes with mixture. Press an almond into the centre. Serve
piled on a dish, garnished with watercress and almonds.

Serves 4

Apple Compôte

METRIC/IMPERIAL

125 g/4 oz sugar
300 ml/½ pint water
1 strip lemon rind or 2
   teaspoons chopped fresh
   ginger

750 g/1½ lb apples, peeled,
   halved, cored and sliced
5 mm/¼ inch thick

Melt sugar and water in thick pan with lemon or ginger. Boil fast for 2 minutes.

Cook apples in the syrup in covered pan over low heat for about 10 minutes until just soft. Serve hot or cold with custard, cream or ice-cream.

Serves 5–6

VARIATIONS: Substitute plums or gooseberries for apple.
   Substitute red wine for water. Add a little lemon juice if too sweet.

Apples with Chocolate

METRIC/IMPERIAL

50 g/2 oz sugar
150 ml/¼ pint water
500 g/1 lb cooking apples,
   peeled and sliced
strip lemon peel

150 ml/¼ pint whipped double
   cream
125 g/4 oz plain or bitter
   chocolate, grated
little green colouring

Boil sugar and water 5 minutes. Add apples. Simmer over low heat, covered, until soft. Cool.

Add green colouring. Pour into a glass dish. Spread with cream and sprinkle chocolate thickly on top of the cream. Serve with sponge biscuits.

Serves 4

Baked Apples Monique

METRIC/IMPERIAL

4 large cooking apples, cored
25 g/1 oz butter or margarine
50 g/2 oz sugar
1 teaspoon grated lemon rind
  and/or fresh chopped ginger
  or pinch ground ginger

2 tablespoons double cream
2 tablespoons redcurrant or
  blackcurrant jelly

Make a slit round the middle of the apples with a sharp knife, to prevent them splitting.

Fill the apples with small pieces of butter, sugar, lemon and/or ginger. Bake on top shelf of preheated oven (160°C/325°F, Gas Mark 3) for about 30 minutes.

Pour some cream into each apple. Put a large spoonful of the reducrrant or blackcurrant jelly on top and serve. Hand more cream separately.

Serves 4

NOTE: It is a good idea to sit each apple on a round of buttered bread before baking to absorb any juices.

Pear and Gingerbread Upside-Down Pudding

METRIC/IMPERIAL

25 g/1 oz butter or margarine
75 g/3 oz honey
2–3 ripe pears, peeled, halved
   and cored
50 g/2 oz butter
50 g/2 oz golden syrup
2 level tablespoons sugar
1 egg

150 g/5 oz flour
½ level teaspoon baking soda
2 level teaspoons each ginger
   and cinnamon
150 ml/¼ pint milk
pinch salt
4 maraschino cherries

In a cake tin, 18 x 7 cms/7 x 3 inches, melt the butter or margarine and honey and stir to mix. Brush sides with melted butter. Arrange pears in tin, cut side down with cherry in centre of each.

Cream butter, syrup and sugar. Beat in egg.

Sift the flour and dry ingredients on to a piece of paper. Then sift again into the creamed mix in the bowl, using a strainer or sieve.

Stir with a metal spoon. Add enough milk to make a thick batter. Pour into the cake tin over the pears. Bake on middle shelf of a preheated moderate oven (180°C/350°F, Gas Mark 4) for 30–40 minutes, until the centre feels firm. Turn out on to a hot dish.

Serve hot with cream, ice-cream or custard, or cool for 10 minutes in the tin and turn out on to a rack and serve cold.

Serves 4

Pears with Rice and Chocolate Sauce

METRIC/IMPERIAL

600 ml/1 pint water
125 g/4 oz white sugar
125 g/4 oz pudding rice
150 ml/¼ pint evaporated milk
3–4 pears or apples, peeled
  cored and halved
75 g/3 oz plain or bitter
  chocolate

4 level tablespoons dark brown
  sugar
1 level tablespoon cocoa
150 ml/¼ pint water
1 teaspoon black treacle
orange sections or few
  cherries

Boil water with white sugar to make a syrup.

Simmer rice in 300 ml/½ pint water over low heat, covered, until the water is absorbed and the rice tender. Stir in the evaporated milk.

Cook fruit on lowest heat in the syrup, covered, until just tender. Cool in the syrup, then drain, retaining syrup.

Add some of the syrup to the rice to sweeten it, but not too much to make it too soft. Pour into a glass dish and chill.

Boil next five ingredients together in an open pan. Then simmer for about 20 minutes until it becomes syrupy. Cool.

Arrange the halved fruit on top of the creamed rice, pour the chocolate sauce over, just covering the pears and not the rice.

Arrange orange or cherries between the pears, or round the edge of the dish.

Serves 4

NOTE: The chocolate sauce will keep in a well-washed screw-topped jar. A can of creamed rice can be used. Stir in a tablespoon of ground almonds if it is not quite thick enough to support the fruit on top.

Apricot Tid-Bits

METRIC/IMPERIAL

1 large orange, preferably
  seedless
250 g/8 oz dried apricots
250 g/8 oz demerara sugar

Extract orange juice. Mince orange shells alternately with the apricots using a medium mincing plate attachment from a food processor.

Melt orange juice and sugar together in a thick pan over low heat. Add orange and apricot. Cook slowly, stirring often to make a stiff paste. Cool a little.

Turn on to board thickly dusted with granulated sugar. Cut into pieces, roll into balls with wet hands. Shake balls in a polythene bag with granulated sugar until well coated. Dry on cake rack.

Makes 750 g/1½ lb

VARIATION: Use only 175 g/6 oz sugar and stir in 2 tablespoons of condensed milk. Mould into apricot shapes. Press a line down the middle with a spoon. Brush one side lightly with a little carmine or cochineal. Press in a stalk of angelica.

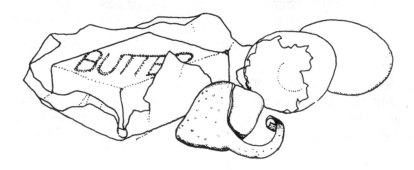

Apricots Milanaise

METRIC/IMPERIAL

250 g/8 oz dried apricots,
   soaked overnight in 150 ml/
   ¼ pint orange juice and
   150 ml/¼ pint water
50-75 g/2-3 oz sugar

2 eggs, separated
150 ml/¼ pint double cream
25 g/1 oz almonds, split and
   blanched
few angelica leaves

Cook apricots for 10 minutes or until soft, adding a little more water if needed. Liquidize apricots and juice in a blender, or rub through a nylon sieve. Combine apricot pulp while hot with sugar and egg yolks. Cool.

Fold in whipped cream and then stiffly beaten whites. Pour into glass dishes. When set, decorate with almonds and angelica leaves.

Serves 4

NOTE: This sweet is also good for food value as it contains iron and vitamin C.

Ambrosia

METRIC/IMPERIAL

250 g/8 oz dried apricots,
   soaked overnight
300 ml/½ pint water
125 g/4 oz honey
grated rind and thinly sliced
   flesh of 2 large seedless
   oranges

1 fresh coconut, grated
25 g/1 oz granulated sugar

Cook apricots gently in soaking liquid until tender. Add honey. Cool.

Mix most of orange rind with sugar.

Arrange oranges, apricots and coconut in layers, with the juice. Top with coconut, sprinkled with orange rind and sugar. Chill. Serve with cream or ice-cream.

Serves 4

Baked Bananas

METRIC/IMPERIAL

1 kg/2 lb very ripe bananas,
   peeled
50 g/2 oz butter, melted
50 g/2 oz demerara sugar

1 heaped tablespoon syrup or
   honey
2 tablespoons lemon juice

Butter a shallow ovenproof dish. Fill with bananas. Cover with melted butter. Sprinkle sugar on top. Trickle over the syrup or honey and lemon juice.

Bake on top shelf of a preheated moderately hot oven (180°C/350°F, Gas Mark 4) for 20–30 minutes. Brown a little under the grill. Serve hot with cream.

Serves 4

VARIATIONS: Add 1 tablespoon rum, just before serving.
   Use concentrated orange juice instead of lemon. Top with grated fresh coconut and then dredge with icing sugar.

Banana and Orange Cream

METRIC/IMPERIAL

2 ripe bananas
1 tablespoon lemon juice
1 large can evaporated milk

1 can frozen orange juice
glacé cherries or chocolate
   'scrolls'

Mash bananas and lemon juice with a stainless steel or plastic fork. Add milk and orange juice and beat well together to make a smooth cream. Rub through a nylon sieve to remove any lumps, or liquidize in a blender.

Pour into five or six small glass dishes, chill. Decorate with glacé cherries or 'scrolls' of plain chocolate.

Serves 5–6

Prune Creams

250 g/8 oz large prunes or
   1 x 500 g/16 oz can prunes,
   soaked overnight in 450 ml/
   ¾ pint water or cold tea
lemon jelly crystals dissolved in
   150 ml/¼ pint water as
   directed on the packet

1 egg white
squeeze lemon juice
25–50 g/1–2 oz sugar
whipped cream or almond
   cream
little grated plain chocolate

Simmer prunes gently in covered pan until tender. Cool. Remove stones and sieve. Measure purée and liquid and make up to 450 ml/¾ pint with water.

Melt jelly crystals in water over low heat. Stir into purée mixture. Add lemon juice and sugar, if needed. Cool. Fold in stiffly whisked egg whites.

Pour into glass dish or small dishes to set and decorate with cream and chocolate or pour into a wet basin or mould to set. Turn out on a dish and decorate with piped rosettes of cream and grated chocolate.

Serves 4–5

NOTE: If using a blender liquidize hot stoned prunes and liquid with jelly crystals and water, to a smooth purée. Add lemon juice and sugar, if needed. Fold in whisked whites and proceed as above.

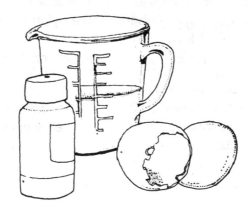

Sugar-Iced Fruits

METRIC/IMPERIAL

175 g/6 oz granulated sugar
150 ml/¼ pint water
pinch cream of tartar or
  1 teaspoon lemon juice

375 g/12 oz red, white and
  black currants, grapes,
  stoned apricot halves,
  orange sections, firm whole
  strawberries

Melt sugar and water with cream of tartar or lemon juice in a thick pan over low heat. Boil to 160°C/320°F, test with sugar thermometer. Remove from heat.

Using tweezers, dip bunches of currants into hot syrup for a few seconds. Take out carefully and put on an oiled dish or plate to cool.

Serve piled on an attractive dish, decorated with washed blackberry or currant or strawberry leaves.

Serves 4

NOTE: Remaining syrup can be used to make a compôte of fruit (see Apple Compôte, page 227).

Creamy Lemon Cheese

METRIC/IMPERIAL

250 g/8 oz cottage cheese
1 large lemon, rind and juice
1–2 tablespoons castor sugar
1 egg yolk
25 g/1 oz unsalted butter,
  softened

few walnuts, chopped
4 teaspoons raspberry or
  strawberry jam

Blend all ingredients together in a liquidizer or in a bowl, using a wooden spoon, until light and creamy.

Spoon into four glasses. Chill. Garnish with a spoonful of strawberry or raspberry jam and nuts. Serve with sponge fingers or biscuits.

Serves 4

Almond Cream Mould

METRIC/IMPERIAL

75 g/3 oz almond cream
1 tablespoon honey or sugar
600 ml/1 pint water
4 level teaspoons Gelozone

1 tablespoon orange flower
    water (optional)
25 g/1 oz blanched almonds
few glacé cherries

Whisk almond cream, honey and 300 ml/½ pint water, warm together to make almond milk.

Mix Gelozone with 300 ml/½ pint cold water. Bring to boil. Simmer 3 minutes. Cool. Add almond milk and orange flower water.

Pour into a wet bowl or mould. Chill. Turn out into a glass dish. Decorate with almonds stuck into the mould, and halved cherries. Serve with a fruit syrup such as rosehip or blackcurrant syrup; or stewed or canned damsons.

Serves 4–5

Crème de Luxe Ury

METRIC/IMPERIAL

250 g/8 oz strawberries, fresh
    or frozen
125 g/4 oz raspberries, fresh or
    frozen
250 g/8 oz cottage cheese
1–2 tablespoons brandy

2 tablespoons sweet white
    wine
50 g/2 oz castor sugar
150 ml/¼ pint whipped cream
little cochineal colouring

Blend fruit, cheese, brandy, wine and sugar in a liquidizer for 1 minute. Alternatively, mix fruit and cheese and mash through a sieve with a wooden spoon into a basin. Blend in brandy, wine and sugar.

Fold in cream. Add colouring. Fill glasses and chill.

Serves 6

Autumn Cream

METRIC/IMPERIAL
250 g/8 oz cottage cheese
250 g/8 oz blackberries, fresh
  or frozen
1 tablespoon sugar

2–3 tablespoons blackcurrant
  syrup
vanilla to taste

Liquidize cheese, most of fruit, sugar and syrup. Add vanilla to taste. Alternatively, mix cheese and most of fruit and mash through a nylon sieve or strainer into a bowl. Blend with syrup, sugar and vanilla.

Serve in glasses, chilled and garnished with a few blackberries on top.

Serves 4

NOTE: This sweet is rich in vitamin C.

Strawberry or Raspberry Cream

METRIC/IMPERIAL
275 g/9 oz strawberries or
  raspberries, fresh or frozen
250 g/8 oz cottage cheese
2 tablespoons castor sugar
few drops of vanilla

few drops carmine or
  cochineal
whipped cream, if liked
few chopped nuts

Put 250 g/8 oz fruit, cheese and sugar into liquidizer. Blend for 1–2 minutes. Add vanilla to taste. Alternatively, mix 250 g/8 oz fruit and cheese together. Rub through nylon sieve or strainer, into a bowl, using a wooden spoon. Mix in sugar and vanilla to taste.

Colour with carmine or cochineal, using a skewer, dipped into the colouring. Serve in glass dishes, chilled, garnished with a little whipped cream and remaining fruit or nuts.

Serves 4

Apricot Cream

METRIC/IMPERIAL
250 g/8 oz cottage cheese
125 g/4 oz dried apricots,
   soaked overnight in 300 ml/
   ½ pint canned orange juice
   or 250 g/8 oz canned
   drained apricots and
   1 tablespoon frozen orange
   juice

2–3 tablespoons castor sugar
   or soft brown sugar
few sugared almonds

Liquidize cheese, apricots and sugar in a blender.

Alternatively, mix apricots with cheese and mash through a nylon sieve into a bowl, mix in sugar to taste.

Serve the cream in glass dishes or cups, chilled and garnished with Sugared Almonds (see page 249).

Serves 4

Mixed Fruit Creams

METRIC/IMPERIAL
250 g/8 oz cottage cheese
150 g/5 oz double or single
   cream
25–50 g/1–2 oz sugar

1 x 500 g/16 oz can fruit
   cocktail, drained
2 tablespoons sweet sherry
few cherries

Blend or liquidize together cheese, cream and sugar. Fold in fruit cocktail and sherry. Pour into small dishes to set. Chill. Decorate with cherries.

Serves 4

Pashka or Russian Cream 1

METRIC/IMPERIAL

375 g/12 oz cottage cheese or
curd cheese
150 ml/¼ pint sour cream
125 g/4 oz unsalted butter
125 g/4 oz castor sugar
125 g/4 oz almonds, chopped
or ground

125 g/4 oz mixed, candied
orange and lemon peel,
finely chopped
250 g/8 oz raisins, stoned or
seedless
vanilla essence to taste
few glacé cherries

Mix cottage cheese and cream thoroughly. Blend in other
ingredients.

Drape a piece of butter muslin over a pudding basin and fill
with the mixture. Cover with muslin and place a saucer with a
1 kg/2 lb weight on top to press out surplus moisture.

Stand in a cold place for about 12 hours. Turn out on a dish,
garnished with glacé cherries. Serve, cut in wedges, with
single cream.

Serves 6

Pashka 2

METRIC/IMPERIAL

250 g/8 oz cottage or curd
cheese
1 x 300 g/10 oz can
evaporated milk
grated rind and juice of small
lemon
50 g/2 oz castor sugar

50 g/2 oz ground almonds
125 g/4 oz mixed stoned
raisins and sultanas
50 g/2 oz dried apricots, cut in
small pieces
150 ml/¼ pint single cream
1 tablespoon rosehip syrup

Press the cheese through a strainer or sieve if necessary to
make it smooth. Combine cheese, milk, lemon rind and juice,
sugar and almonds to make a thick cream. Stir in dried fruit.
Pour into glass dish. Chill. Serve with cream, mixed with
rosehip syrup.

Serves 4

Eastern Yogurt

METRIC/IMPERIAL

2 cartons natural yogurt

1 tablespoon coarsely
   desiccated coconut or
   grated fresh coconut

1 level teaspoon castor sugar

1 tablespoon lemon juice

50 g/2 oz seedless raisins

little grated lemon rind

Mix all ingredients together, put in a screw-topped jar or covered dish and chill. Let stand at least 1 hour before serving to allow flavours to develop.

Serves 3

Lemon Yogurt

METRIC/IMPERIAL

600 ml/1 pint natural yogurt

2 tablespoons double cream

grated rind and juice of
   1 lemon

1–2 teaspoons castor or icing
   sugar

Beat all ingredients together in a bowl and put in small pots. Let stand in a bowl of warm water for 30 minutes to set. Chill in refrigerator.

Serves 4

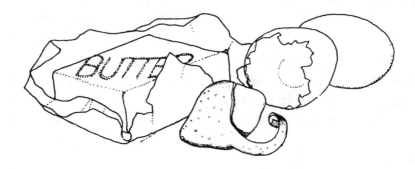

Muesli 1

METRIC/IMPERIAL

300 ml/½ pint natural yogurt
75 g/3 oz raw rolled oats
1 tablespoon honey
3 tablespoons evaporated milk
250 g/8 oz tart apple, coarsely
  grated
1 lemon, grated rind and juice
1 banana, sliced

1-2 tablespoons brown sugar
50 g/2 oz nuts, grated or milled
2 tablespoons double cream
few fresh or frozen
  strawberries or raspberries
canned or fresh oranges,
  peaches or apricots
whole nuts for garnish

Mix together yogurt, oats, honey and milk. Let stand at least 1 hour. Stir in next six ingredients. Pile in a dish; garnish with fruit and nuts.

Serves 4

Muesli 2

METRIC/IMPERIAL

75 g/3 oz rolled oats
150 ml/¼ pint water or milk
150 ml/¼ pint orange juice
50 g/2 oz sultanas
1 large cooking apple, cored
  and coarsely grated
2-3 tablespoons sweetened
  condensed milk

1 tablespoon honey
grated rind and juice of
  1 lemon
50 g/2 oz hazelnuts or cashew
  nuts, milled or chopped
cream (optional)
slices various fruit

Mix together oats, liquid and sultanas. Leave 1–2 hours or overnight. Stir in apple, condensed milk, honey, lemon rind and juice and nuts. Serve in a dish, topped with cream and fruit.

Serves 4

Orange Yogurt

METRIC/IMPERIAL

600 ml/1 pint natural yogurt
2 tablespoons double cream
1 teaspoon grated orange rind

1 level tablespoon sugar
1 orange peeled and diced
(50-75 g/2–3 oz)

Whisk yogurt, cream, orange rind and sugar together. Pour into warmed pots. Add some orange pieces to each pot. Cover.

Stand the pots in a saucepan of warm water, covered, to set again. Keep in refrigerator.

Serves 4

VARIATIONS: Substitute drained canned pineapple, apricots, raspberries and strawberries; or frozen or fresh strawberries, raspberries, blackberries for the orange.

Cream Yogurt

METRIC/IMPERIAL

600 ml/1 pint natural yogurt
150 ml/¼ pint double cream

Stir the yogurt and cream together. Pour into small pots and chill. Serve with honey, brown sugar or rosehip syrup. Also delicious and nutritious served with thin honey and milled walnuts or wheatgerm.

Serves 4

NOTE: This mixture can be used instead of soured cream.

Blackcurrant and Almond Paste Tart

METRIC/IMPERIAL

for almond paste:
250 g/8 oz ground almonds
175 g/6 oz castor sugar
175 g/6 oz icing sugar
1 egg
1 tablespoon lemon juice
almond and vanilla essence to
  taste

for filling:
375 g/12 oz fresh or frozen
  blackcurrants or 1 x 500 g/
  16 oz can blackcurrants
125 g/4 oz sugar
150 ml/¼ pint water
1 level tablespoon arrowroot

For almond paste, mix almonds and sugars to a firm paste with lemon juice and eggs. Flavour with essence.

Cook blackcurrants with sugar and water over low heat. When soft drain in nylon strainer. Keep juice. Cool.

Roll out paste to 2.5 mm/⅛ inch thick on a board dusted with icing sugar. Line a deep sandwich tin. Trim edges and decorate. Roll out scraps and cut into strips.

Fill case with blackcurrants.

Boil the syrup. Add arrowroot blended with a little cold water. Boil to thicken. Cool a little, pour some over the fruit (but not too much) and arrange strips of paste in a lattice on top.

Bake on top shelf of a preheated moderate oven (180°C/350°F, Gas Mark 4) 15 minutes. Serve cold, with cream.

Serves 4

VARIATION: Cheaper than almond paste, soya paste is made by mixing together 150 g/5 oz full fat soya flour, 175 g/6 oz castor sugar and 175 g/6 oz icing sugar with 65 g/2½ oz unsalted butter or margarine adding enough sherry and water to make a firm paste and also almond and vanilla essence to taste.

Chocolate Mousse

METRIC/IMPERIAL

125 g/4 oz plain or bitter
  chocolate
1 tablespoon water, orange
  juice or rum
2 large eggs, separated

2 tablespoons single cream or
  top of milk
little orange rind mixed with
  sugar or instant coffee or
  cocoa

Melt chocolate in a bowl, standing in a saucepan of hot water. Remove from heat. Using a wooden spoon, stir in water, juice or rum and egg yolks. Fold in stiffly beaten whites, using a metal spoon.

Fill five small pots or glasses nearly to the top. Chill. Top with single cream and decorate with orange rind and sugar, coffee or cocoa.

Serves 5

Zabaglione

METRIC/IMPERIAL

6 egg yolks
6 level tablespoons sugar
150 ml/¼ pint Marsala wine or
  Madeira

Whisk egg yolks and sugar together until white. Place bowl over a pan of hot water on stove and whisk in the wine gradually, until the mixture thickens. Pour into warmed glasses and serve at once.

Serves 4

NOTE: To make Zabaglione Ice-cream, fold 150 ml/¼ pint whipped cream into cooled Zabaglione and chill in freezer or ice-box. Spoon into glasses and decorate with cherries.

Sweet Fluffy Omelette

METRIC/IMPERIAL

2 eating apples, peeled and diced small
1 ripe banana, sliced
1 orange, peeled and cut in sections
1 teaspoon rum or liqueur if liked

3 large eggs, separated
2 level tablespoons castor or soft brown sugar
15 g/½ oz butter
little icing sugar
little grated chocolate

Collect prepared fruit in a bowl. Add rum or liqueur.

Beat egg yolks and sugar until creamy, then fold in stiffly beaten whites. Pour over fruit. Stir lightly with handle of wooden spoon.

Melt butter in 20–25-cm/8–10-inch frying pan. Pour in the egg and fruit mixture. Cook over low heat until bottom is set. Put pan under low grill and cook until top is lightly set and golden brown. Loosen edges with round-bladed knife and slip out onto a hot dish. Serve dusted with icing sugar and sprinkled with grated chocolate.

Serves 4

Cheesecake

METRIC/IMPERIAL

125 g/4 oz flour
50 g/2 oz margarine
water to mix
1 can skimmed, condensed milk
2 eggs, separated
rind and juice of 2 large lemons

25 g/1 oz butter, softened, or
  margarine
50 g/2 oz sultanas
1 digestive or ginger nut
  biscuit, crushed

Prepare a pastry case (see Danish Quiche, page 106). Fill with bread crusts and bake on top shelf of a preheated hot oven (200°C/400°F, Gas Mark 6) for 15 minutes.

Beat together in a bowl, condensed milk, egg yolks, rind and juice of lemons and softened butter. Stir in sultanas. Fold in beaten whites.

Put filling into cooked pastry case and sprinkle a few biscuit crumbs over top. Put in moderate oven (180°C/350°F, Gas Mark 4) for 40–45 minutes until set. It is done when it feels firm in the centre. Turn off heat and leave to cool in the warm oven with the door open.

Serve cold with cream.

Serves 4–5

Cornflake Crisp

METRIC/IMPERIAL

50 g/2 oz butter or margarine
125 g/4 oz cornflakes
25 g/1 oz brown sugar

little grated orange or lemon
  rind

Melt butter, stir in cornflakes, sugar and grated rind and heat through. Press into a shallow tin and allow to cool. Cut into pieces when set.

Serves 5

Danish Red Jelly

METRIC/IMPERIAL

600 ml/1 pint blackcurrant
   juice or mixed raspberry and
   blackcurrant juices drained
   from canned or stewed fruit
   or diluted from bottle

2 rounded tablespoons
   cornflour or arrowroot
25 g/1 oz almonds, blanched
   and split
150 ml/¼ pint whipped cream

Blend cornflour with a little cold juice to a thin cream. Boil remaining juice and stir into cornflour mixture. Return to pan and bring to the boil. Boil for 1 minute. Pour into a dish and chill to set. Decorate with almonds stuck into the jelly and rosettes of whipped cream.

Serves 4–5

Nutty Brittle

METRIC/IMPERIAL

125 g/4 oz sugar
150 ml/¼ pint water
50 g/2 oz sesame or sunflower
   seeds or 75 g/3 oz nuts

Melt sugar and water in a thick pan over low heat without stirring. Boil until temperature reaches 155°C/310°F. Tip in seeds or nuts.

Pour on to oiled baking sheet or marble slab. Mark in squares. Leave to set. Break while still warm.

Makes 250 g/8 oz

Coconut Crisps

METRIC/IMPERIAL
1 large fresh coconut
salt

Pierce coconut and remove milk. Remove shell. Using a potato peeler, cut coconut flesh into thin strips. Spread coconut strips in single layers on baking trays. Bake in very slow oven (130°C/265°F, Gas Mark ½) for 1 hour, until crisp and light brown.

Sprinkle with salt while hot. Stored in air-tight tins, they will keep for 3 weeks. Crisp again if necessary in a warm oven.

Serves 6–8

NOTE: For white crisps, bake at 115°C/240°F, Gas Mark ¼.

Peppermint Chews

METRIC/IMPERIAL
2 rounded tablespoons syrup
125–175 g/4–6 oz dried
  skimmed or whole milk

few drops of peppermint
  essence

Melt syrup in a saucepan. Cool a little. Work in as much dried milk as is needed to make a stiff paste. If mixture becomes too stiff, warm pan a little. Add peppermint essence. Turn on a board dusted with granulated sugar and milk powder. Cool.

Pull off pieces and shape into long rolls or balls. Leave to harden (they may need re-shaping). Cut into cushions with scissors. Wrap in waxed paper and store in tin.

Makes 250 g/8 oz

VARIATIONS: Instead of syrup use black treacle, malt extract or honey.

Peanut Butter Candies

METRIC/IMPERIAL

2 rounded tablespoons peanut
   butter, smooth or crunchy
2 rounded tablespoons honey

1 teaspoon lemon juice
2–3 rounded tablespoons
   dried milk powder

Blend peanut butter, honey and lemon juice together with wooden spoon. Work in enough milk powder to make a dry, stiff paste.

Shape to a square 1 cm/½ inch thick on a board dusted with a little milk powder. Leave to set 1 hour. Cut into 1-cm/½-inch cubes, or shape into balls and decorate by pressing in nuts or stoned raisins or shape into a roll 5 cm/ 2 inches in diameter. Wrap in foil, chill and slice.

Makes 125 g/4 oz

VARIATIONS: Mix in grated orange rind or vanilla essence to taste.
   Add 1 heaped tablespoon of desiccated coconut and a few drops of vanilla essence. Shape on a board dusted with coconut.
   Add 1 tablespoon fine chopped walnuts or hazelnuts.
   Add 1 rounded teaspoon cocoa powder and vanilla essence.
   Substitute 1 rounded tablespoon each of syrup and black treacle for honey.

Sugared Almonds

METRIC/IMPERIAL

50 g/2 oz split, blanched
   almonds
1 drop almond essence

1 tablespoon milk
50 g/2 oz castor sugar

Combine almonds, essence and milk in a bowl. Put the just-moistened almonds in ovenproof dish. Dredge with sugar. Brown under low grill for about 20 minutes, shaking frequently. Cool.

Makes 125 g/4 oz

Creamy Candies

METRIC/IMPERIAL

⅓ cup milk
1 rounded tablespoon
   margarine or butter (40 g/
   1½ oz)
125 g/4 oz sugar
1 teaspoon vanilla essence

25-40 g/1–1½ oz chopped
   walnuts
25 g/1 oz wheatgerm
50–65 g/2–2½ oz skimmed milk
   powder

Melt milk, butter and sugar together in a thick pan over low heat without stirring, until it bubbles all over surface. Boil for 2 minutes to 115°C/235°F. Cool.

Add vanilla, nuts and wheatgerm. Stir in enough milk powder to make a thick paste. Beat well until creamy. Quickly turn into oiled, shallow tin. Mark into squares. Or drop by teaspoonfuls. Leave to stand 1 hour. Cut into squares or if in teaspoonfuls remove from tin.

Makes 250 g/8 oz

VARIATIONS: Substitute brown sugar for white. Instead of walnuts and vanilla use 2 tablespoons peanut butter and little grated orange rind. Instead of wheatgerm, stir in 2 level tablespoons cocoa.

Salted Cashew Nuts and Peanuts

METRIC/IMPERIAL

250 g/8 oz nuts
2 tablespoons oil
½ level tablespoon sea salt

Fry nuts in oil over low heat, stirring frequently until pale brown or bake in a tin with oil in a very moderate oven (160°C/325°F, Gas Mark 3) for about 30 minutes. Drain on kitchen paper. Shake with salt in a paper bag.

Makes 250 g/8 oz

NOTE: These nuts will keep, stored in a screw-top jar.

Fruit Bars

METRIC/IMPERIAL

125 g/4 oz dates, stoned
125 g/4 oz raisins, stoned
125 g/4 oz prunes, stoned
50 g/2 oz brazil nuts and
  walnuts mixed

50 g/2 oz ground almonds
25–50 g/2 oz dried skimmed
  milk
1 tablespoon lemon juice

Put fruit and nuts through a fine mincer. Mix them with almonds, milk and lemon juice, to make a stiff paste. Add more lemon juice if needed. Press onto a sheet of rice paper and cover with another sheet and make a neat block.

Leave overnight to harden. Cut into squares with knife dipped in boiling water. Pack in waxed paper and store.

Makes 500 g/1 lb

VARIATIONS: Dates, with dried apricots, raisins, nuts, grated orange rind and juice.
Figs, dates, raisins, and nuts with lemon rind.
Prunes, raisins, currants, honey and chopped fresh or preserved ginger.
Dates, raisins, prunes and nuts with 50 g/2 oz chocolate.

Drinks

Housewife's Cocktail

METRIC/IMPERIAL
150 ml/¼ pint orange juice
1 egg
1 teaspoon honey or sugar

*2 tablespoons sherry or dash
of brandy*

Whisk or blend all ingredients together and pour into a glass.

Serves 1

Mexican Chocolate

METRIC/IMPERIAL
1 rounded tablespoon cocoa
300 ml/½ pint hot water
*1 tablespoon sugar or
equivalent sweetener*

*150 ml/¼ pint strong coffee
(preferably freshly brewed)
cream to taste*

Boil cocoa, water and sugar together. Whisk. Whisk in coffee.
Add cream to taste.

Serves 2

NOTE: This drink is rich in iron and niacin.

Tiger's Milk

METRIC/IMPERIAL

150 ml/¼ pint orange juice
150 ml/¼ pint milk
1–2 level tablespoons yeast
  powder
1 tablespoon soya or corn oil

1–2 tablespoons instant milk
  powder
1 scant teaspoon vanilla
  essence

Liquidize or whisk all ingredients together. Store in closed jar in refrigerator.

Serves 1

NOTE: This can be stored in the refrigerator – the flavour improves on keeping.

VARIATION: Increase amounts dried milk and yeast if liked.
    Use 150 ml/¼ pint concentrated orange juice and 150 ml/¼ pint pineapple juice.
    Add an egg.

Blackcurrant Vermouth

METRIC/IMPERIAL

150 ml/¼ pint blackcurrant
  syrup or juice from canned
  fruit

150 ml/¼ pint dry vermouth
lemon slice
ice cubes

Mix, chill and serve.

Serves 1

NOTE: This drink is rich in vitamin C.

Chocolate Orange Milk Shake

METRIC/IMPERIAL

150 ml/¼ pint concentrated
  orange juice
450 ml/¾ pint milk

1–2 tablespoons chocolate
  powder
1 egg

Whisk all ingredients together. Serve cold.

Serves 3

Index